LET THE CRABGRASS GROW

H. ALLEN SMITH'S SUBURBAN ALMANAC

Books by H. ALLEN SMITH

MR. KLEIN'S KAMPF

LOW MAN ON A TOTEM POLE

LIFE IN A PUTTY KNIFE FACTORY

LOST IN THE HORSE LATITUDES

RHUBARB

LO, THE FORMER EGYPTIAN!

LARKS IN THE POPCORN

WE WENT THATAWAY

PEOPLE NAMED SMITH

MISTER ZIP

SMITH'S LONDON JOURNAL

THE COMPLEAT PRACTICAL JOKER

THE REBEL YELL

THE AGE OF THE TAIL

WRITE ME A POEM, BABY

THE PIG IN THE BARBER SHOP

DON'T GET PERCONEL WITH A CHICKEN

WAIKIKI BEACHNIK

LET THE CRABGRASS GROW

Selected by H. Allen Smith

DESERT ISLAND DECAMERON

With Ira L. Smith

LOW AND INSIDE

THREE MEN ON THIRD

let the crabgrass grow

H. ALLEN SMITH'S
SUBURBAN ALMANAC

ILLUSTRATED BY DONALD MADDEN

PUBLISHED BY

BERNARD GEIS ASSOCIATES

DISTRIBUTED BY RANDOM HOUSE

First Printing

Library of Congress Catalog Number 60-10125

Designed by Edwin H. Kaplin

Manufactured in the United States of America by
American Book-Stratford Press, New York

Contents

SUMMER

FALL

WINTER

Introduction

[It's Not Nice to Have a Man
Around the House]

THIS is my husband's twenty-third book. In most of the others he has found reason to write at some length about me. In this book, which is a reflection of the kind of life we lead in the suburban countryside of North Westchester, it is only natural that he should now and then refer to me and tell stories about me. I won't charge him with writing untruths; I won't say that he deliberately exaggerates; I prefer to say, as Mrs. Sam Snead once said of her husband, "He just remembers big."

After all these years, then, it is a pleasant thing to get my turn at the typewriter. This is not so much an introduction to a book as it is an introduction to my husband. I think I know him pretty well.

First of all, I would like to say that he is a cotquean.

No matter how it sounds, the word means something else. The big Webster defines it: "A man who busies himself with affairs properly feminine." Another wordbook says that a cotquean is an "apron husband." I am sorry I ever learned about this latter definition because it has shown me how sad my plight really is—I have, at my house, a *two*-apron husband. He has one apron for the kitchen and one for outdoors. They are not interchangeable.

The woman whose husband gets up early each morning, showers and shaves and eats a fast breakfast and then rushes off to his work, to be absent from home all during the long golden hours of the day—that woman is immeasurably blessed by the gods. There may be times when she *thinks* it would be nice to have a man around the house on a full-time basis, but she really doesn't appreciate just how lucky she is. Solitude, I can assure her, has its good points.

My husband, being a free lance writer, is at home twenty-four hours a day, seven days a week, fifty-two weeks a year. (No wonder he has time to compile an almanac!) What I mean to say is that he is *underfoot* that long. I have borne this cross for the twenty years that he has been working at home, and I am constrained to say that it is no way for people to live. Sometimes I actually yearn for the good old days when I didn't know where he was and worried myself sick because he was late coming home and hadn't telephoned.

WHEN we bought our house in the country fifteen years ago I kept an eye peeled for the proper arrangement of rooms, for the thought was constantly in my mind that I have a stay-at-home husband. And when we found a house with quarters over the garage, separated from the main building by a long breezeway, I knew I wanted it. When I said, "Oh, look! You could have your office, your study, clear over here, away from everything, so nobody would disturb you," I knew what I was doing. He could have his office, his study, clear over there, away from everything, away from *me*, so *he* wouldn't be disturbing *me*. At least, that's the way I visualized it.

I understand that there are writers and artists and composers who isolate themselves during their creative periods, even locking themselves into soundproof studios, and that they will never brook interruptions short of the house catching on fire. My husband is not like that. If someone, or something, does not interrupt his work within a reasonable length of time, he will emerge from his lair and *go looking for an interruption.*

He meddles in my affairs ("affairs properly feminine") from morning to night. There is never any such thing as "a surprise for dinner tonight" at our house. All wives enjoy an occasional fancy fling in the kitchen, whipping up something special for the weary and hungry husband who will be home on the 6:57. It can never happen in my house. My cotquean haunts the kitchen when anything is being cooked. He pokes into things, tastes things, demands to know what has been put into things. "You got any orégano in this?" he'll call out. Or if it's not orégano, it's sweet basil or bayleaf. If I put in basil, he says it should have been bayleaf, and if I put in bayleaf, he says it should have been coriander. And the truth is, I'm quite sure he can't tell the difference between the taste of coriander and the taste of dodder.

An ordinary wife, whose husband is away at the office or the factory, can simply make up her mind what she's going to have for dinner and then cook it. Not me. I have to consult with him. It is necessary that we have a summit meeting before I go to market. I have to take his order. And then I have to ask him if he wants to do the cooking himself and, if not, how he wants it cooked. I might as well be a waitress in a dog wagon.

Once or twice a week he takes over the cooking in the kitchen (he does all of the meat-ruining outdoors) and when this happens I try to find an excuse to get away from the house. Miles and miles away. Beyond the sound barrier if possible. He is a loud-type cook, both from the standpoint of clatter and from the standpoint of howl. He bangs things around and he howls because he cannot locate other things to bang around. He sharpens knives. God, how he sharpens knives! I'm sure that even women who have go-to-work husbands know about this knife-sharpening disease, this grindstone syndrome. My husband howls about dull knives, and then sharpens them, and twelve hours later he howls again and sharpens again. My fingers are growing knotty from scar tissue acquired from handling the razor edges that lay in wait for me in every corner and every drawer of my kitchen. We keep such quantities of Mercurochrome around the kitchen that I'm sure people suspect us of using it in beef stews.

Down through the years he has accumulated a veritable hardware store of his own and installed it in my kitchen. He is daft about jar-openers. He possesses every known gadget for removing lids and caps, but that would not be so bad if it weren't for his practice of always buying two of everything. If he finds a new lid-loosener downtown he buys two of them, on the grounds that one may fail him in a crisis. There are, of course, knife-sharpeners located in strategic spots all over the property, some of them electric, some hand-powered, some to be used only for steak knives (we have two sets of steak knives, one set being, he says, for emergencies) and then in addition to all that, we have one immense and cumbersome grindstone for sharpening scythes. I've never understood why we don't have two of those grindstones, because we have two scythes.

He fancies himself as a mechanical genius, and so he is always tinkering things out of commission. If a thing is already out of commission, he will tinker it into such a condition that even the professionals will be unable to fix it. He doesn't even understand the simple functioning of our clothes washer. The only mechanism with which he is at all familiar is his own defense mechanism. He covers up by charging *me* with being dumb about the washer, clumsy about the vacuum cleaner, ignorant about the oven, all in an effort to conceal his own inadequacy. He is completely thrown by a plain hammer.

I COME now to one of the most horrible manifestations of the Husband Eternally At Home. He snoops on my telephone conversations.

One of the true pleasures of life for the modern woman, no matter how silly it may seem on the surface, is the daily telephone talk with friends. Of course it lasts a long time, for there is much to say. Of course it is frivolous talk—we are not dealing here with Great Conversations featuring, say, Bertrand Russell and David Susskind and Peter Ustinov and Bergen Evans. We are talking about that perfectly normal institution, woman-talk. My husband snoops on it. For quite a few years he refused to have an extension telephone in his office, on the ridiculous grounds that he could not abide interruptions. He spoke of the telephone as being one of the major curses of civilization. Now we have *two* extensions, installed on his order a year or so ago. Whenever I am talking to one of my friends I can usually hear the click as he picks up the receiver in his office. He knows I can hear that click so he doesn't pretend that he isn't on the line. But he does hang on with consummate brass and while my friend and I stubbornly proceed with our chitchat, he puts in punctuation, such as, "Great God!" or a sarcastic, "Can you *imagine* that!" or "Do tell!" or "Will wonders never cease!" If I order him off the line, which is likely, he argues that he is *doing research*, that as a writer he seeks an understanding of the feminine mind. This from an incorrigible cotquean! And when he wearies of his "research" he asks me to please get the hell off the line, that he is expecting an important business call from California. In the last twenty years he has had exactly one important business call from California.

If, by some rare chance, he gets into a period of steady work at the typewriter, I am still far from being my own woman. Just when I begin to feel that my mornings, at least, are free from interference, he'll come striding in a business-like manner over to the house.

"What was the name of that horse-faced woman we met that evening at the Royal Hawaiian?" he'll demand. And when I can't tell him, he'll lose his temper and raise his voice, expressing wonder that he is able to make a living at all, taking into account his wife's brain, which has no memory lobes on it.

Sometimes, yielding to irritability, I recommend that he get into his car and leave the premises for a while. That is, I used to do it. No more. Whenever he leaves the house with no definite destination in mind he almost always heads for the village and buys shoes. I can get him away from the house but he'll come home with more shoes. He has two closets full of shoes. Many of them have never been on his feet since the day they were tried on him at the store.

Or, I could leave the premises myself—go away for days at a stretch. Like fun. One of his chief addictions, in recent years, has been the accumulation of books containing Household Hints. He also collects them out of magazines and newspapers, and he copies others into notebooks after hearing about them from women (I almost said *other* women). He has a passion for discovering spots; in trying to remove the spots, he creates spots that couldn't be removed with cannon fire. If I go away for longer than a few hours, it is almost a sure thing that he'll get out his Household Hints and find a good solid, substantial Hint to keep him occupied.

Once I came home and found the dining room littered with bread fragments and bread crumbs and horrid-looking balls of bread. One of his books had told him that a good way to clean soiled wallpaper is to take half a loaf of bread and rub it over the paper. When I walked in he was working on

[14]

his third half-loaf. He stood there ankle-deep in bread litter and said, brightly, "You should always use a downward motion for best results." When I protested against this idiocy, he countered with a bitterly-worded complaint that I never keep solid loaves of bread in the house, just bread that is already sliced, so that if a man gets the urge to clean the wallpaper, he has to drive all the way downtown to get unsliced wallpaper bread.

Another time he all but destroyed the wall back of the electric range. He installed, or tried to install, a window shade roller behind the grill, with a strip of oilcloth tacked on it, the idea being that this crummy shade could be pulled down during cooking operations, thus keeping grease from sputtering on the wall. "The beauty part of it," he said, "is that when you're through cooking you just roll it up, out of the way." He meant that's what you would do if he had ever got those damn screws to hold in the plaster.

Just a few days ago he crept into the house with approximately two bushels of rhubarb (plus a new pair of shoes) but I caught him before he could do whatever he was going to do. He told me later that the way to make all our aluminum pans clean and shiny is to cook rhubarb in them. Fortunately I know the grocer and when I took all that rhubarb back, he said, "I thought at the time that Mr. Smith was buying a little too much for just two people, but you know how he is sometimes."

Having told all these things about him, there is one important matter remaining to be said. It is exciting to be around him, and it is also fun. This has been especially true during the fifteen years we have been living in the outer suburbs of New York. I think that anyone who reads this book will agree.

Nelle Smith

SPRING

I have a grandson who goes about, day and
night, with an old ragged diaper hanging from
his mouth, and I am a normal citizen in other
respects, too.

—Sayings of Avery

Municipal Affairs

[The Town of Horseless Taverns]

March 21—Now in the month of rain and sleet and bitter
March winds I have determined to put together an almanac
for the amusement and instruction of the multitudes who
inhabit those sections of our land called The Suburbs. Some
residents employ the Spectorsky word and refer to themselves as Exurbanites. Others speak of having A House in
the Country. It is all pretty much the same.

Twelve years have now passed since I produced a book
titled *Larks in the Popcorn.* That book covered the beginning years of our transition from city-dwellers to country
folks. In those dozen years there have been great changes in
the hills of North Westchester. When we first came to our
Dutch colonial house we could stand in our front yard and
see a vast semicircle of hills and valleys spread before us, and
if we looked closely we could see a few houses, or corners
of houses—maybe ten or twelve altogether. Now there are
hundreds.

The biggest town in our neighborhood, and the closest to our house, is Mount Kisco, which is thirty-five miles north of the Island of Manhattan. I have heard a native-born citizen of the town speak of a far distant land which he called Westconsin. And it was a man from the same Westconsin, visiting in Mount Kisco, who made the comment: "Nice country up around in through here."

If the town has a symbol it is the statue of the Indian, known as Chief Kisco, standing in the whirl of traffic on Main Street. He is on a pedestal, rising out of a stone watering-trough, and he was presented to the town many years ago by a citizen of stout prohibitionist beliefs. Engraved on the pedestal are the words: *God's Only Beverage for Man and Beast.* It is said locally that when horses stopped for a drink they read this inscription and took heed of its message, with the happy consequence that a horse has not been seen in a Mount Kisco tavern in more than fifty years.

℃

When we first moved up here, Mount Kisco was a genuine village, reminding me a great deal of the small Midwestern communities I knew as a child. All the ingredients that go to make up the classical American small town were here, plus an additional something that is important. Instead of farmers, the surrounding countryside is thickly populated by a breed known to the natives as Hilltoppers. Some of them are people of means. I mean means. Rich people. And cluttered around their great estates are lesser households occupied by people who commute to New York and who all seem to work for the same company—a firm called The Rat Race.

In recent years we have lost two of our most spectacular Hilltoppers—Tallulah Bankhead and Billy Rose. Tallulah sold her house shortly after she got her first look at a tomato hornworm but she comes back now and then to talk at her old friends; Billy Rose's mansion burned to the ground one night and with it went his pool table, and the loss of the latter so depressed him that he decided to take up permanent residence in the city.

You can loaf along Main Street or Moger Avenue almost any day and see important characters out of the world of television, publishing, heavy industry, welterweight industry, advertising, Wall Street, the art galleries, sports and the theatre. In the supermarkets you might brush pushcarts with Gian-Carlo Menotti or Bennett Cerf or Arlene Francis or even Jackie Gleason. Jackie likes Mount Kisco and leased an estate here one summer and still talks of establishing a high-class restaurant in the village. One evening in a local horseless tavern he struck up an acquaintance with several young men and they invited him over to have a look at the Italian-American Men's Club. The local slickers whispered to each other behind their hands and lured Mr. Gleason into a poker game and somewhere along toward dawn Jackie departed for home, all his pockets stuffed with U.S. currency. When I saw him the next evening he remarked with great seriousness, "I like this town. It's got atmosphere. I may move up here for good." He did buy a house a few miles to the west, a fantastic establishment which some of his friends call The Flying Saucer. Jackie's own name for it is "Reggie's Place."

☺

In recent years the Moral Rearmament group has established its headquarters at the former Hammond estate southeast of town, and now we occasionally get Oriental and Middle East people on the streets, plus the rabbinical students from nearby Yeshiva—bearded young men in flat black hats. The *Reader's Digest*, just two miles south of town (it is *not* in Pleasantville!), draws a steady stream of famous visitors who want to see how it's done, and they too show up on the streets of our village. And the barn theater (where such stars as Henry Fonda and James Stewart got their early training) brings in Broadway and Hollywood notables during the summer months.

The New York Central runs through the town, carrying commuters, and we've had a big grade crossing elimination project on our hands lately. For something over a year it looked as if an H-bomb had fallen in the center of town, but now the job's all finished. The Central's roadbed has been shifted, the depot has been moved and refurnished, sleekly graceful overpasses of steel and concrete are in place and the plaza area has been converted into a handsome and spacious garden.

The whole West Main Street business district had to be torn down to make way for the principal overpass. The displaced merchants moved, for the most part, into spanking new buildings erected along Moger Avenue. An entirely new shopping area was born where there had been nothing but swampland before, and now that long stretch of street is agleam with chrome and glass and fresh paint.

While all this was going on, many of the oldtimers shook their heads sadly. Mount Kisco, they groaned, would never be the same. Too many new people coming in. Too many new Hollywood-style buildings. Too many split-level houses rising in the hills. The flavor was all going out of the place. Why, just look how darn fancy Fox & Sutherland's got!

I had a little of the same feeling. I used to love the classic confusion of the old Fox & Sutherland store on West

Main, where you could buy everything but fresh meat and automobiles. This was the dingy, crowded place where the natives and the Hilltoppers met to shop and get information and argue politics and arrange for baby-sitters and leave their umbrellas and locate a man to wash windows or a girl to type a manuscript. You wanted to buy a phonograph needle and Jack Sutherland would cry out: "Hey, Herman, where's the phonograph needles?"

"Look up front," came the answering shout, "under the color film, the 16 millimeter." And that was where they were. Under the 16 millimeter film, not the 8 millimeter. Got to preserve order. Got to be able to find phonograph needles when they're wanted.

There were all manner of characters around the store. One disreputable old man arrived every afternoon and took his place beside the newspaper table and talked to the customers, always saying the same thing. He'd point to the top headlines on the latest papers and, no matter what they proclaimed, he'd say, "See. Whad I tell ya?" And there was the town's leading practical joker who always chose Fox & Sutherland's as the place to start his rumors. He'd come in and say, in a normal tone of voice, to the man at the cigar counter, "Burnin' like a barn fulla hay. Got fire departments from far away as Ossining." People would edge in, to find out about the fire. "Didn't you hear?" he'd say. "Chappaqua station's burnin' down. Last I heard the roof was gone." In five minutes the story would be all over town and people would be leaping into their cars and roaring off toward Chappaqua to see the burning station.

So when Fox & Sutherland moved into its glittering new building on Moger Avenue there was a general feeling that something pleasant, something homey, had gone out of our lives. They had designed the new store for space and magnificent orderliness. A place for everything and everything in its place. The books here, the magazines there, the records yonder; special cases and shelves for fishing tackle and cameras and Scout equipment and dolls and candy and barometers and snowshoes and tape-recorders and ink and Ping-Pong tables and stamps and leather goods and coonskin caps and golf clubs. The new store has now been going long enough to take on a permanent character. That character is one of ineffable confusion; there is now more space in which to achieve confusion and I'm certain that if you looked under the 16 millimeter film you'd find the phonograph needles, exactly where they belong.

The people of Mount Kisco, then, remain the same as they were before. They still congregate in Fox & Sutherland's and josh one another and trade gossip and shift the merchandise around a little more, so that even Herman sometimes has trouble finding things. Truth is, the town hasn't changed at all, for a town isn't steel and stone and chrome and concrete. A town is people.

Chappaqua, where the station didn't burn down, is a lovely community to the south of us and there are other pleasant towns nearby—Bedford Village and Bedford Hills and Katonah and Armonk and Pleasantville. In some respects, however, the most interesting community in the whole area is North Patent. It reflects a little bit of each of the other villages that surround us. We shall hear more about North Patent.

The Perversity of Nature (Namely Crabgrass)

March 25–For some time I've kept a file devoted to observations under the general heading, "Perversity of Nature." For example, there's a small patch of lawn across from the breezeway and every spring for three years I've been trying to get some grass to grow properly on it. I seed it and water it and lime it and fertilize it and tote bushel after bushel of leaf mold out of the woods and scatter on it. The grass comes up in little tufts, if it comes up at all, but over on the pavement–a three-inch layer of Colprovia that cost me a fortune–a whole crop of crabgrass is growing like mad. Some of the crabgrass, in fact, grows so energetically that it pushes up lumps in the Colprovia before it breaks through. So I get out the sprayer and load it with weed-killer, mixed so strong that it almost withers the brass nozzle, and I saturate the grass that is defacing my beautiful pavement. Does it kill the crabgrass in the pavement? Hell, no! But it really puts the finishing touches on my small patch of lawn. Solution? Why, let the crabgrass grow! Yes, that's it. Just let the crabgrass grow.

> I met a fellow today who said there are only eight sounds that can be put together to make a popular song and that all possible combinations of those eight sounds have now been used up. Good God I hope so.
>
> *—Sayings of Avery*

Back Talk

[My Wife Nelle]

March 28–Mark Twain once described his mother as a kindly and compassionate soul who always warmed the water before drowning the kittens. My wife Nelle is much the same way. Notwithstanding the gender in which she is trapped, she is a *good* creature.

An introduction to a book is customarily written after the book itself is finished. But when she is on the subject of *me*, Nelle is all full of tweeters and woofers and she couldn't wait; her little essay, which leads off this almanac, was written before I started putting the book together.

I admit that it must be trying on the patience of a woman to have her husband around the house twenty-four hours a day. Nevertheless it is my belief that the world would be a better place if all husbands stayed home every day, for the simple reason that wives need steady supervision. Steady and firm. Left to themselves, unwatched,

[24]

they will permit a man's property to decline and disintegrate and the kitchen knives will grow so dull they wouldn't cut lard.

Most husbands already know about the telephone conversations their wives have with other women, and they know also that these conversations can take on a slight patina of silliness. Certainly I eavesdrop on them. I have listened to my wife and Evelyn S—— talk on the phone for one hour and fifty-three minutes without either of them uttering a single reasonable sentence. Meanwhile, in the kitchens of both houses the knives grew duller and grease spattered on the wall back of the stove and the aluminum ware took on a heavy greenish tinge for lack of rhubarb. I snoop on those conversations because I am, in a way, a social scientist with a profound interest in the behavior patterns of all living organisms. If I came upon two wart hogs, standing face to face in a jungle clearing and grunting steadily at each other, and they continued this grunting for an hour and fifty-three minutes, I would stay with them, hoping always that I would learn something important about the psychology of the wart hog.

When it comes to my shopping in the food markets, I want to make it known that I am a friend and benefactor of grocery clerks and butchers. They are the most abused and put-upon class of people in the United States. They are at the mercy of women like my wife, and I am convinced that all women are like my wife. There is a pretended camaraderie existing between grocery clerks and their women customers: I hear them joking back and forth, and I observed the butchers and the clerks making pleasant remarks about the weather and even commenting favorably on the hair styles of their customers. This is all play-acting. The women do not like the clerks, because they consider the clerks to be crooks and swindlers and givers of short change. For their part, the clerks and butchers, behind their pretended gaiety, are choking back wild and untrammeled profanities, and I know that they would dearly love to pat the ladies on their hairdos with the flat side of meat cleavers. My wife suspects every person involved in retail trade of trying to cheat her, and by strong implication she makes it clear to them that she considers them to be crooks. It is inconceivable to her that a man could offer to sell her anything that wasn't somehow faulty, rotten to the core and overpriced.

"Are those eggs fresh?" she always demands. Her tone clearly says that those eggs are not fresh, that it is the grocer's practice to stock rotten eggs. She dislikes ordering groceries by telephone, preferring to be on the scene where she can detect the swindling. But she keeps dishonesty to a minimum by saying distinctly, over the telephone: "I want a *nice* head of lettuce. And, let me see. Do you have any *nice* strawberries? Yes, two boxes if they're *nice*." That same word, "nice," dominates all grocery lists which I have to carry to the stores. It has become so inextricably involved with her shopping that I once stopped in a hardware store, at her request, and asked the man for a *nice* can of varnish.

I think perhaps that she scored a near-hit on me when she mentioned shoes. It just happens that I like the fellow who runs the shoe store and enjoy talking to him, and I don't believe in going into a man's store without buying a little something. Anyway, a weakness for shoes is not such a bad thing. *She* has a mania for vacuum cleaners. At the present moment she has *four* vacuum cleaners. She uses one of them exclusively for cleaning the basement and I suspect that she sometimes vacuums the front yard. Not long ago I was away on a brief trip and when I got home she had acquired a brand new vacuum cleaner, the latest model, one of those that climbs up a flight of stairs without help and then puts itself to bed. I asked her why in the name of time she had bought still another one, and she said she had to have one to clean out the bags of the other three. In other words, she'll vacuum the downstairs with Vacuum No. 2 and then she'll use Vacuum No. 4 to vacuum out the bag of Vacuum No. 2, and then she'll take Vacuum No. 4 out to the incinerator and empty *its* bag by hand. This thing has a dangerous potential that I'd rather not think about.

℃

My wife charges me with not understanding the clothes washer. In turn I charge her with purveying slipshod directions. A marvel of spoken confusion would be a recording of her voice instructing someone how to get to our house. It is a wonder to me that more recipients of her directions are not found floating face downward in the Hudson River, eight miles above Albany. But as to the washing machine, her orders to me just before she leaves the house, go like this:

"Now remember. Soon as you hear it stop its present cycle, run down and flip it over."

I nod, and continue my philosophical ruminations, or my knife sharpening, and finally I'm aware of the fact that the washer had stopped its present cycle. Now, what was it she said to do? Run down and flip it over. I run down. There it stands, pale and quiescent, waiting to be flipped over, nothing but a far-away hum discernible. I reach my hand out, then withdraw it, and reach it out again, and then

I yell. I yell with nobody to hear me but the powers and principalities of the air: "Flip *what* over! ! !"

There was a time, long ago, when I thought that working at home was the greatest thing that could happen to a man. I considered myself to be one of the fortunate few—the men who don't have to put on neckties and jackets and rush for subways or commuter trains or buses. I really felt sorry for those others. Then one day I found myself in a small group of men who were my neighbors. They were all commuters, and I somehow felt superior toward them and spoke smugly to them about the horror of their daily routine.

They heard me out and then one of them spoke for the group.

"You don't commute?" he asked.

"I certainly do not," I said with pride.

He looked at me curiously for a long time, his eyes widening.

"You mean," he finally said, "you have to stay home all day, every day, *with your wife?*"

Perhaps he had a point. If so, it isn't important right now because my own mood is one of deep humility. I confess that for twenty years I have been writing somewhat caustically of my wife's manners and misdemeanors. She was entitled to a turn at bat. She had every right to search for the chinks in *my* armor. Even if there aren't any.

A Flaw in Our Suburban Civilization

April 1—An advertising man of my acquaintance stopped by tonight for a visit and we got to talking about country living versus city living. He said that he is thinking about returning to the city. He has one major complaint against the country.

"When we lived in New York," he said, "and I got into a fight with my wife, I always did the same thing. I'd stomp out of the apartment, go down to the street, walk to the corner, go into a saloon and stand there and drink. Maybe even get drunk. You ever notice the men lined up at the bars in those places? Half of them are cooling off after fights with their wives. They don't want to talk—they just stand there, gripping their drinks, their jaws set, fire in their eyes. They drink for an hour or two and then it's safe for them to go home again. I always thought that was one of the nice things about civilized living. But out here, goddamit, whenever I get in a fight with my wife, I stomp out of the house and get in the car and I have to drive clear the hell and gone all the way to Ridgefield to find a saloon to sulk in. By the time I get there, and get the car parked, and make it to the bar, I've almost forgotten what I got mad about."

> Learning to be a millionaire is like anything
> else; it takes a lot of practice, the same as
> swimming or golf or playing the piano. You
> just keep at it, keep doing it over and over,
> and finally you get the hang of it.
> *—Sayings of Avery*

Introduction to a Neighbor

[The Admirable Avery]

April 5–It is time for an introduction to my neighbor Avery. Other people pay little attention to him and look upon him as a dullard and a mope. In my opinion he towers over all his neighbors. He is an original. He comes at me with the most unexpected propositions. I remember the time last month, for instance, when he stopped by my house and asked me what kind of poison I thought would be suitable for use on a welcome mat.

Coming from anyone else, the question would have been disquieting and I'd have edged my way around the room to the fireplace, handy to the poker. But over a period of fifteen years I've grown accustomed to the off-beat genius of Avery in the field of technological chaos. "What kind of a welcome mat is it?" I asked.

He said it was an ordinary brown fiber mat which he keeps at his front door and which has the word "Welcome" dyed into the fibers in green. He told me that about a week back the blue jays discovered it. They would move in shortly after dawn, four or five of them, squawking and shrieking as they ripped at the cocoa fibers. Within two days they had pulled the mat to pieces and carried off the shreds. Avery went down and bought another one and put it on his porch. The next morning the jays went to work on it. The racket they made, of course, had been rousing him from his bed. He'd come downstairs in his pajamas, uttering sentiments that would have bruised the heart of John J. Audubon. He'd get a broom and fling open the door and go at the blue jays, and the blue jays would take off in the direction of Mount Kisco. But the moment Avery got back into bed, they'd return and resume their noisy annihilation of the welcome mat.

By this particular morning Avery's personal fibers were as shredded as the fibers of the two door mats. His peculiar genius would not permit him to think of an easy solution to his problem. He never once thought of taking the mat inside the house before going to bed at night. Nor did it occur to him that buying a rubber mat would abate the nuisance. No. He was buying a third fiber mat and he was going to saturate it with poison.

As it turned out, he really didn't want me to recommend a poison; he already knew which type would blend best into cocoa fibers. All he wanted of me was that I go downtown to the drugstore and buy the poison for him.

"I don't know why I should be this way," he told me, "but I'm sensitive about that type of shopping. I've never been able to walk into a drugstore and ask for poison. I get the feeling that the druggist is looking me over suspiciously —has me figured for a man who's going to slip rat poison into his wife's soup; either that or commit suicide."

[31]

I'm usually inclined to go along with his projects, but I'm the same way about buying poison, so I argued him out of it. "I'm surprised at you," I said, "wanting to poison those blue jays. You—a bird lover. You—after all you did for those baby robins."

℃

Avery's experience with robins occurred just about a year ago. His cousin, a lumber dealer from Ohio, was spending a week at Avery's house. There was a robin's nest in a young maple near the kitchen door and the two men made a discovery. In the nest were three newly-hatched baby robins. Avery and his cousin watched the nest for a day and a half and then arrived at the unhappy conclusion that the mother robin had been taken by a hawk or a boy with a BB gun. They became co-mothers to the baby robins.

They started out with bread crumbs, but the babies wouldn't touch them. They went out after dark with flash-lights and collected nightcrawlers and draped them around the rim of the nest. The sub-fledglings reacted with horror in the presence of these worms, apparently thinking they were interplanetary monsters. They hugged their skimpy wings against their bodies and cowered away from the nightcrawlers. Avery's cousin said, "The worms are too big. We need littler ones." So they dug in the ground and got littler ones, and the babies spurned them.

"I've heard or read somewhere," said Avery, "that the way it works is, the mother pre-digests the . . ."

"Now, just a minute," said his cousin. "I, for one, am not going to pre-digest anything, most of all I'm not going to . . ."

"Wait!" said Avery. "I've got it!" They went downtown and bought a can of pablum and an eye-dropper. They stood on kitchen chairs beside the maple tree and tried to feed the pablum to the birds, but the birds wouldn't take it. Apparently it was too dry. So they tried other baby foods—special preparations of apple sauce, bananas, and so on. No luck.

And then, all in a single night, the three baby robins died. Avery was quite depressed over it and that day he drank a little more than was his custom. His cousin left for home and in the evening Avery came over to my house to tell me the whole unhappy story. He said: "I've reached the conclusion that one damn robin is smarter than two grown men."

☺

It seemed to me inevitable that those robins should perish, for Avery is a man with a consuming desire to do things, and he can't do anything. He reminds me, in a way, of a character in one of O. Henry's stories, a man named Kearny, who could never do anything right. This Kearny said of himself:

"Everything I get into goes up in the air except a balloon. Every bet I ever made I lost except when I coppered it. Every boat I ever sailed on sank except the submarines. Everything I was ever interested in went to pieces except a patent bombshell that I invented. Everything I ever took hold of and tried to run I ran into the ground except when I tried to plow."

That's Kearny, and that's also Avery. There's a contractor in our community who speaks of certain people as being "mechanically clined." Avery is not clined mechanically. In fact that is the major element of his genius—he is, in my estimate, the least mechanically clined person alive on this earth. Ideas and projects and inventive schemes boil and bubble out of his mind—ideas that sound remarkably sensible when first stated. Yet he is incapable of ever executing them. He is a man with only one knack—a positive talent for misfeasance with tools. His wife chews at him about his consistently maladroit performance in the presence of a small job to be done, and his friends rag him about it; but the nagging and the ragging only serve as a goad, a challenge, and he'll try anything. I think the garage man who serves us both sums him up best when he says, "That Avery! He'd try to milk a he-goat through a sieve." And the hardware store people are delighted with him. They count it a dull day when Avery fails to pay them a call.

Some of his friends have recommended to Avery that he give up trying to be his own handyman, that he hire an odd-jobs man to come around one day a week. He argues that he only confounds confusion whenever he engages a workman, and then tells about the stone wall.

At first he tried to build the masonry wall by himself. Within two days he had created a shambles, as everyone knew he would. So he shopped around and found a stone mason who would come over on a weekend and do the job at three dollars an hour.

That same weekend Avery's two small grandchildren came for a visit. The stone mason was just getting himself organized when the children approached him and asked him to give them a ride in his wheelbarrow. He loaded them in and wheeled them back and forth across the lawn several times. Now they demanded that he take them out for a ride on the highway. He balked, and went to Avery about it, and Avery said of course not. The children, when told they couldn't ride any more in the wheelbarrow, set up a fearsome caterwauling. Avery tried to effect a compromise—

he would shove them around in the wheelbarrow while the mason worked on the wall. But they wouldn't hear of that. They wanted to ride in the wheelbarrow while it was being propelled by the nice man who talked funny. The children, to be sure, won the argument. And the stone mason spent the better part of Saturday and Sunday trundling those kids around the property, and back and forth on the highway. When it came time for him to quit on Sunday, he told Avery: "I feel kinda guilty about it, but I still got to charge you three bucks an hour. It was harder work with them kids, and more nerve-wracking." The stone wall was never finished—was never really begun.

As I have suggested, Avery is quick to admit his shortcomings. His bumbling, he feels, is an incurable affliction and he is resigned to it. When he does complain about it, he lays the blame on Fate, or the natural perversity of inanimate objects with special reference to himself as victim, or illiteracy among manufacturers. He insists upon buying new gimmicks and gadgets and, with the manufacturer's instruction sheet spread out before him, trying to assemble them himself. Invariably he botches the job and invariably he sits down and writes an indignant letter to the manufacturer and invariably the letter contains a single devastating sentence:

"Why don't you twerps learn the proper use of the English language!"

A Note on Chickens

April 6–When we first moved to the country there were a hundred thousand questions to be settled and each question seemed to have a hundred thousand answers. Should we plan on chickens? There was a fine chicken house which, with a brief cleaning, would be ready for occupancy, and a sizeable fenced chicken yard next to it. Chicken culture on a small scale was certainly suggested, since the war was still on, and if you got a cube steak the size of a slice of bread you felt like having a home movie made when it was put on the table. Yes, we had better plan for a small flock of chickens. Even though I had been an apprentice chicken-picker as a boy, I knew nothing about the raising of them, so I acquired some chicken books and began studying. I read about chickens for two days and then telephoned Mount Kisco and arranged to have carpenters convert the chicken house into a tool shed. I wanted no part of chickenkind. In the first place, the biological angle was confusing to me—the exact algebraic relation of rooster to hen to egg to chick. I have got so I can understand the human way of things fairly well, but it's a little different with chickens, and tends to confuse me just as all this business about mules and jennies and jacks and mares and donkeys has always confused me. Moreover, I learned some understandable facts which militate against chicken husbandry. They get spells of biting one another in the behinds. They attract rats. They stink. They get coccidiosis. The dictionary says coccidiosis is "Infestation with protozoans of the order of Coccidia, esp. of the genus Eimeria (syn. Coceidium)." Sounds even worse than that to me. Anybody, or anything, that gets coccidiosis, I don't want to be the doctor. So I have a tool shed.

Lo, the Plowman!

April 9–The deep-rooted feeling that the plowman has for the good earth has been celebrated in prose and poetry for centuries. A literary friend of mine who has a country place nearby is a great reader of novels about the soil, and from those books he has acquired the notion that the spiritual relationship between the farmer and the field is a truly beautiful thing.

Just recently this man told me he heard tractor noises near his house and went out to investigate. He found a man in overalls plowing a field adjoining his property. My friend went out and hung on the fence and watched the plowing for a while, and noted with pleasure that the man riding the tractor had a genuine farmer look about him. After a time the farmer pulled up near my friend, shut off his engine, lit up a cigarette, and they started talking.

"What are you going to plant here?" asked my friend.

"Couldn't say," responded the man on the tractor. "Don't have any idea. My job is to plow it, and then I've got to come back and harrow it, and after that I'm through. I don't know what they're gonna plant and I don't give a damn—all I gotta do is to get 'er plowed and harrowed."

Salesmanship

April 9–Now in the early springtime the seed catalogues and the shrubbery salesmen come upon us. A few days ago an elderly man arrived at my house, sedate of manner, aristocratic bearing, clipped white mustache, conservative dress. He thought I ought to buy some oriental trees from his company. I finally convinced him I have more trees than I can cope with. He was walking toward his car on the driveway when another thought occurred to him. He turned and came back and said, "Perhaps you could use some material for a new book." I had to tell him that I have less use for that than I have for trees.

There's such a thing as too much point on a
pencil.

—Sayings of Avery

Boys

[Sporting Life on West King Street]

April 12—Last evening, having been invited to dine at seven
at the home of the Schuyler Huffs, I arrived precisely at
seven to find myself, as usual, distressingly early. The Huffs
hadn't even begun their toilette so they settled me down in
the living room and vanished upstairs. I was busying myself
with a copy of *Variety*, seeing who was N.Y. to L.A. and
who was L.A. to N.Y. and who was N.Y. to Europe, when
a juvenile apparition suddenly appeared before me, making
clanking noises. It was Little Sky, the ten-year-old of the
Huff menage. He had on a coonskin cap and a fringed
leather jacket. Around his middle was a webbed belt from
which were suspended a Scout axe, a hunting knife, and a
small skillet, a compass, a pedometer, a flashlight, and an instrument which I judged to be a moose call. There was a
bulky rolled pack on his back and slung from his shoulders
were a canteen and a portable radio.

"Well," said Little Sky, "I guess I'll hit the trail."

"You headed for the Canadian Rockies?" I asked him.

"Nope," he said. "Just camping out all night with Billy Peckham. We camp out once every spring."

"Where are you going to do this camping out?"

"Well," he said, lowering his head a trifle. "Billy's mother won't let him stay outdoors all night, so, well, we're going to camp out in Billy's bedroom."

He seemed to be sagging under his equipment so, even though I knew the Peckhams lived just two doors away, I offered to drive him to the frontier. He gave me a scornful look. "I prefer to hike it," he said, and went clanking out the door.

❦

I sat there thinking of all that paraphernalia he was toting and I shook my head inwardly. (Shaking the head inwardly is a thing I must have learned in my own youth. The inside parts of the head rotate slowly from side to side while the outside of the head remains perfectly stationary. It sometimes hurts.) And I cast my thoughts back to that Pleistocene era when I was ten years old. Immediately I found the answer to an old and vexing question—why do I, even today, insist on saving bits of string, old pieces of leather, scraps of lumber, and bent nails? Why is it impossible for me to throw away a wheel off an old garden cart?

When I was ten I lived on West King Street in a central Illinois town. There were twenty-five or thirty boys in the two blocks that comprised our realm and each of us, in order to participate in sports, had to develop the skills and instincts of the hawk, the beaver and the pack rat. We probably spent more time in searching for and manufacturing sports equipment than we spent in our actual games. No matter where we went, no matter what important errand

[40]

we were performing, our eyes were constantly alert for certain articles that were almost essential to existence. Sports for us began at the junk pile.

An old discarded shoe was a prize beyond valuation. The tongue was the most valuable part of the shoe, furnishing material for at least two sling-shot pouches. String was as important to us as candy. Lumber scraps and old nails were hoarded as if they were ebony and silver, and to find a wheel of any kind—even the iron band off the hubcap of a farm wagon—was to find bliss.

We had few "boughten" things. Every boy had a jack-knife, which he usually got for Christmas, and every boy had a bag of marbles, including an aggie, a steelie and a lot of commies. (In my time I've associated with a lot of commies, but I've always had them under my thumb.) This wealth was kept in fairly equitable distribution through trading. Negotiations over the swap of, say, one knife with a busted handle for one steelie and ten commies would sometimes last an entire week. It was a more obdurate and unsentimental form of commerce than you'll find even at the Flea Market in Paris. I've long since lost track of the King Street boys, but I feel certain that some of them grew up to become either merchant princes or highly successful confidence men.

So far as the sporting life was concerned we really lived off the land. We seldom went out deliberately to hunt for equipment—we were forever on the prowl for it. Just beyond our home territory lay open country—a crick where we swam and fished, wooded areas where we went hickory-nutting, and fields where we occasionally passed an hour or two snatching grasshoppers. Snatching grasshoppers can be a more strenuous sport than badminton and serves to develop both the *latissimus dorsi* and the *pectoralis* muscles.

There is not a great deal of purpose in catching grasshoppers, no more so than in mountain-climbing. After a grasshopper is caught, you close your fist over him, leaving his head sticking out and, squeezing him gently, you say, "Spit tuhbacca juice er you die!" The grasshopper obliges by spitting tobacco juice and you let him go.

Whenever we were in the woods we occasionally cut prongs for sling-shots. Our sling-shots were made from a tree fork, two lengths of rubber cut from an old inner tube, bits of string and the pouch fashioned from the tongue of the old shoe.

Quite frankly we used our sling-shots to kill birds. Usually we only shot at sparrows, which we called spriggies and which we understood to be anti-social varmints. We fancied ourselves as marksmen but to be candid about it, something over two-and-a-half tons of stone were shot at spriggies for every spriggie hit.

One of our most common sports was hoop-rolling. Not the brand they practice at Wellesley. Our hoop-rolling was a boy-sport that seems to have been indigenous to the Middle West. The "handle" was usually made of lath—a long piece with a short piece nailed crosswise at the bottom, forming an inverted T. This handle was employed to keep a small wheel upright and moving, and the best wheels were the spoked and rubber-tired variety taken off old go-carts. The game may sound dull, but it wasn't. We could keep a wheel going as fast as we could run, uphill or down, or we could maintain it in an upright position while walking slowly behind it. There were periods when we never took a step outside the house without our hoops traveling ahead of us, even going to church.

☺

Nowadays whenever I see a kid whirling a yo-yo, which may have cost a dollar and a half, I think of the shining hours I spent swinging buckeyes. On West King Street we had no superstitions about buckeyes. We knew that some of our elders carried them in their pockets to ward off evil. We had heard the saying: "No man has ever been found dead with a buckeye in his pocket." And we had heard that carrying a buckeye was a specific against both rheumatism and hemorrhoids. (Hemorrhoids!) But we had no concern with rheumatism or hemorrhoids and even less with death, so we used our buckeyes for sport. We'd fasten a buckeye to either end of a string about three feet long. Then we'd hold the string at the middle and set the buckeyes to whirling in opposite directions. Now and then we'd engage in contests to determine which boy could keep his buckeyes whirling for the longest time. I can remember that Donnie Etherton one day kept his buckeyes going for two hours and fifteen minutes and for a week afterwards was unable to use his right hand for scratching himself. There were some boys who could perform intricate maneuvers with their hoops, using one hand, while keeping their buckeyes whirling with the other. I think such boys were freaks of nature, kin to the man in the circus who can stand on his index finger.

Of course we made our own kites—three thin strips of wood which we covered with newspaper, using a paste made of flour and water, and a tail of varicolored rags tied tastefully together. A real sporty kid was one who covered his kite with the Sunday funny paper. Kite flying, to be sure, involved the use of lots of string and each of us spent the entire winter gathering it. We always wound it on a stick, using a figure-eight motion, and a single stick of kite string might consist of more than fifty pieces knotted together. A boy who had a ball of boughten string with no knots was most fortunate because he could send "messages" and little paper parachutes up the string to his kite.

String was most useful, too, in the fabrication of our baseballs. We'd simply wind the string into a tight ball and then cover it with two or three layers of bicycle tape. Our pitchers seldom threw anything but "drops." Major league baseball has never been quite satisfactory to me for the reason that the pitchers never throw a drop. I suppose the sinker ball is the same as a drop, but it doesn't sound the same to me.

We built scooters, using old roller-skate wheels, and most of us made our own sleds (usually with an assist from our fathers), employing for runners the metal strips that came off wagon bodies.

We played mumbly-peg (not mumblety-peg) by the hour. We played shinny with clubs cut from trees and a syrup can for a puck. The shinny games grew more interesting and more lethal as, from constant walloping, the can shrank in size until it was a dangerous metal projectile not much bigger than a hen's egg.

❦

Many of our sporting pursuits were, in fact, quite hazardous. Each tree and each telephone pole in our neighborhood had been climbed more times than the Matterhorn. It seems to me, on reflection, that I spent more time in trees than Tarzan. We played follow-the-leader which usually involved first climbing up on things, such as sheds and embankments and poles and trees, and then jumping off. No paratrooper ever took ground-shocks greater than came to us in follow-the-leader.

Sometimes in the evenings we played crack-the-whip, a

simple exercise in erosion of the human body. I can only remember the times when I was end-man on a line of ten or fifteen boys, and how the whip would be cracked and I'd be sent flying across the fields as if I'd been shot from a cannon. I'm reasonably convinced that I broke through the sound barrier years before anybody dreamed of the jet age.

Also in the evenings we played a multitude of other games, such as chalk-the-rabbit, duck-on-a-rock, run-sheepie-run and Indian wrestling—games known to the kids of other sections of the country but often known under different names. All in all, we kept in fine physical trim. We watched our diet, subsisting on such things as green apples dipped in salt, and the pungent tops of certain weeds. We never needed rubdowns; every boy in our group was certain to get a licking at home once or twice a week and these were not tame affairs—they kept the muscles toned up.

And then after a while the King Street boys grew older and our thoughts turned to the profound mystery of girls and we grew corrupt and decadent and seemed to prefer playing postoffice to swinging buckeyes and chalking the rabbit and jumping off sheds. I've always thought that those were splendid and memorable days. I mean the days when we gave up slingshots in favor of girls.

Items from a Countryman's Notebook

April 17–Speaking for myself and reflecting the opinion of many others, it is a poisonous experience to look at yourself on a television screen and listen to the sound of your own voice. You lose all faith in humanity.

[45]

* * *

Television commercials get better all the time. Just recently I saw one in which the husband is shown arriving home from work. He finds his wife haggard and distrait, stumbling around the smoke-filled kitchen where she has just burned the steak to a cinder. The husband takes in this awful scene then turns and faces the camera and says: "You know what the trouble is here? My wife uses the wrong laxative."

* * *

Charles Darwin wondered if music has any effect on plants, so he engaged a trombonist to play to a row of beans for several hours each day. I don't know how the experiment came out.

* * *

I dearly wish I had hold of the man who, twelve years ago, sold me a gallon jug of corn oil. Each year I grow perhaps twenty hills of corn, and use the oil to fight off earworms. The other day I looked at the jug and found that I have enough of the oil left to last me two thousand years. I've forgotten who sold it to me. I wouldn't throttle him, but he'd end up well lubricated. Inside.

* * *

Rick Barns tells me about an elderly German workman who came to the Barns place to do some odd jobs. He and Rick were tearing down the old stone wall, and they got talking about its great antiquity. Rick told the workman that it was a very old wall, perhaps a hundred and fifty years old. The German delivered himself of a slight snort and then said, "Is not old wall. In my country we've got walls a thousand years old." Having said it, he realized that he had been guilty of a kind of impolite nationalistic bragging, and he felt the need to correct himself, to make Rick feel better about the whole thing, and so he said, "But these *stones* the same age."

Dr. Ferdinand Wake, who has the eye of an eagle, the heart of a lion, the hand of a woman and the paunch of a gourmand, tells me of a local businessman who came to him recently with an unusual complaint. "Doc," he said, in all seriousness, "my spit don't stick." Cross-examination by Dr. Wake elicited the information that the man licks stamps and puts them on envelopes and they promptly curl up and in the end he has to get out the paste pot. He was certain that something dreadful was happening to his metabolism, or some such thing. Dr. Wake finally convinced him that it was the glue that wasn't sticking.

------◆------

Westchester Economics

April 30–Not far from our home is the residence of a prominent doctor, a specialist whose practice is in New York City. He is a man of considerable wealth and he lives out here because his hobby is gardening. During the spring and summer he spends at least one day a week in overalls and blue denim shirt working among his flowers. He has one of the finest gardens in this area.

One day he noticed a big black automobile drive slowly past his grounds while he was at work in the garden. A stiffish matron was driving the car and she stared hard at the doctor as she passed. After a while the car came by again, and again she stared. The third time around the matron stopped the car and got out and approached the doctor.

She glanced all around to make certain that no one was in earshot and then asked, "Are you happy with this job?"

"Yes, ma'am," said the doctor, removing a dirty old hat.

"Would you consider changing jobs?" she asked.

"No, ma'am, I wouldn't," he said.

"I'll give you," she said, "fifty cents an hour more than you're getting here—no matter how much it is—if you'll come and work for me. You look like a man who knows his business."

He still resisted, shifting from foot to foot, turning his hat in his hands. She demanded to know *why* he would spurn such a handsome offer.

"Well ma'am," he said, "it's like this. On *this* job they let me sleep with the madam."

> In this era of the ghosts, my neighbor Smith is
> what is known as a do-it-yourself writer.
> –*Sayings of Avery*

I Told Them So . . .

[The Bracketts and the McCords]

May 8–It's really astonishing how wise I am about so many
things and how people pay no attention to my counsel and
advice. People like the Bracketts and the McCords who just
got back a couple of weeks ago from a vacation. I tried to
warn them but they just laughed at me. One of these days
I'm going to stop solving the problems of the human race
and see if I can't get my own life straightened out.

The Bracketts and the McCords are all about the same
age, hovering close to forty, and they always seemed to be
interested in the same sort of things. They had been close
friends for six or seven years. The four of them played
bridge every Friday night. About once a month they'd have
an evening together in the city and every year in the spring
Freddie Brackett and Pudge McCord went on a week's fishing trip in the Berkshires.

This spring they had decided, for the first time, to take
their family vacation together. I was over at the McCords'
the night last month when they were winding up their plans.

They told me they were going to take the Brackett car because it was heavier and roomier. They had road maps spread out on the dining room table and they indicated that they were going to wander around in Virginia and the Carolinas and maybe see the cherry blossoms in Washington. There was much excited talk about Williamsburg and Charleston and the Skyline Drive and Myrtle Beach and Kitty Hawk and Monticello, and a small argument about whether the last-named was pronounced Monti-*sello* or Monti-*chello*. And Pudge McCord had already started talking in a broad Southern accent. Pudge has a reputation for being quite a wit.

I issued my warning in a good-natured way, as if I were kidding. I asked them if they realized that they were begging for trouble. Pudge said: "Great day in the mawnin', Cunnel, suh, what on earth you got in yo' haid?"

"By the time you get back," I said grinning, "there's a good chance you won't be speaking to each other."

They laughed uproariously and ridiculed the very thought of any trouble between them. Good Lord, they were old friends, tried and true. They knew one another, they understood one another, they always had fun together whatever they did.

So I just smiled and let them go.

℃

They were gone the full two weeks and they were back home another week before I heard anything from them. Then one evening last week the Bracketts stopped by my house.

"Well," I asked, "how was the big trip?"

"Wonderful," said Freddie. "Absolutely wonderful."

"It was a dream," said Marge.

"You mean that it worked out all right—the four of you together?"

"Oh, certainly," said Freddie. "We got along all right. Great people to travel with, Pudge and Evvie."

"Now, Freddie," said Marge, "let's not overdo it. Let's be honest about it. There *were* a few little things."

The "few little things" began to come out. It seems that Pudge had continued talking with a Southern accent. It was very funny, they said, when they were at home, but when he began using it on every Southerner he met, it turned into a source of embarrassment. Every nice restaurant they went into, Pudge would stand at the entrance and declaim to the head waiter, in a voice that could be heard all over the room: "Ah sho hopes y'all got grits, Ah sho cain't git along widdout mah grits!"

Four days of this and the Bracketts decided they'd had enough. "After all," Marge told me, "some of these places were quite dignified, with nice people. I'll admit it was kind of funny the first time he pulled it but after that, every time he went into that grits routine I felt just like disappearing through the floor. So I told Freddie he had to say something to Pudge about it."

Freddie, it appears, did speak to Pudge about his Southern talk. He tried to be tactful. "It's a real funny deal, Pudge, when you pull it up North," he said, "but if I were you I wouldn't do it down here. These Southerners are pretty touchy and I don't think your little act amuses them."

Pudge pretended to take it in good grace but he was actually pretty sore about being told to cut the comedy. He didn't talk much, in any accent, during the next twenty-four hours. And he reverted to his Southern talk only once, when they were at Monticello. He was standing on the veranda of Jefferson's home. A dozen or so tourists were wandering around the yard. Pudge placed one hand inside his jacket and raised the other aloft and in ringing tones announced: "Mah pappy fit de wah so's people would be free! Ah mean evvabody, includin' me!"

"Imagine!" said Marge. "Right in front of all those people, in that sacred place! Honestly!"

"It was pretty bad," Freddie agreed. "But I was willing to forget it. Except that afterwards he wouldn't talk much at all in a conversational way—just certain goofy phrases he'd use, over and over and over."

"It was maddening," said Marge.

It appears that they'd be riding along through the lovely countryside when Pudge would suddenly say, "She snew and she blew." Ten or fifteen minutes later he'd say it again. The Bracketts insisted that he said "She snew and she blew" five hundred times if he said it once. And there was one other phrase he kept repeating. Whenever anybody, in casual conversation, employed the word "almost," Pudge would say, "Almost ain't is." For example, Freddie at the wheel would say, "Almost hit that rabbit." And Pudge would say, "Almost ain't is."

"He just kept it up," said Freddie, "all day long and all evening long. We went to a movie in some town in South Carolina and a character on the screen said, 'It's almost three o'clock,' and this crumb McCord yells out, 'Almost ain't is!' I had to grit my teeth sometimes to keep from telling him to shut his face."

"He got over it, though," put in Marge. "That is, he quit saying those things. But that was after Freddie and Evvie got into the fuss about tipping."

☺

Before they started they had worked out an arrangement on finances. Freddie Brackett was to pay all the bills. Evvie McCord was to keep a notebook and enter every expenditure in it—food, lodging, gas, oil, everything. Then when they got home they'd check Evvie's book with Freddie's deficit and split up fifty-fifty.

"I've always been real fond of Evvie," Freddie assured me, "but she's the penny-pinchin'est dame I ever saw in my life. When I travel I like to travel in a little style. I believe in tipping a waiter twenty per cent. Well, it started in a restaurant just outside Richmond. We had a fine dinner there, cocktails before and a bottle of champagne with the meal. The whole deal came to around twenty-six bucks. So when we got up from the table I slipped a five-spot under my plate. When we got outside Evvie wanted the bad news. She always called it "the bad news." Every time she took that damn notebook out, she'd say, 'Well, what's the bad news?' So I told her twenty-six bucks and a five-buck tip. She let out a holler you could have heard in Baltimore. She said that in her opinion two bucks was plenty. Three at the most. She said things were a lot different down South from what they are in New York. She even threatened to go back inside and ask our waiter for two dollars change. She said maybe I was John D. Rockefeller but Pudge wasn't, and I got good and sore for a few minutes. Well, sir, I never had a real comfortable meal after that. I could tell she was just sitting there waiting, like a hawk, keeping an eye on me to see how big a tip I left. We had lunch one day in a hotel dining room in Charleston and I shoved three half-dollars under the plate, and I'll be darned if that crazy dame didn't pick up my plate and count the money before she left the table. There's a limit to what a man can put up with."

"Now, Freddie," Marge broke in. "Don't get all upset

again. I'm a little on Evvie's side. You know very well that I've always said you tip too much. But I didn't know Evvie was so downright stingy. It sure came out on this trip."

"It usually does," I said quietly, but they acted as if they didn't hear me.

❧

A few days ago I figured out an excuse to call on the McCords. After we got settled down in their living room, they assured me that the trip had been splendid, perfectly splendid. I didn't mention having seen the Bracketts and asked how they were.

"Well," said Evvie, "to tell you the truth we haven't seen them since we got back. We've all been so busy, you know, catching up on this and that."

"Nice guy, Freddie Brackett," said Pudge. "But I'll tell you one thing about him. That bird has yet to learn how to drive an automobile. I sat next to him in the front seat the whole trip and I'll tell you I'm crippled in both legs from pressing against the floorboard. In the first place, I think he's half blind. In the second place, he doesn't know anything about the fundamental rules of the road. And do you think he'd let *me* take the wheel for a while? Not him! Not once on the whole trip. He gets out in a car like that and he puts on the ironman act. Tireless! Mountain of strength! Listen, I happen to know about that guy. He's got a bum stomach, makes him sick about half the time. I could see him turning sort of gray and time after time I'd try to get him to let me drive a while, but he'd just put a big sickly smile on the gray face and say he felt strong as an ox."

"Now, Pudge," put in Evvie, "I don't think you ought to quibble about a thing like that. After all, we agreed to take his car and we agreed that he'd do the driving till he got tired. He insisted he wasn't tired. I could tell he was worn out, just from looking at the back of his head, but he said he wasn't. Let's be fair to Freddie."

"I suppose you're right," said Pudge, "but I still don't like his style of traveling. Here we were on a vacation. I believe in being leisurely about a vacation trip. Relax. Take it easy. Enjoy yourself. Get up in the morning when you feel like it. Decide on a general direction and take off and wander. But not those Bracketts! Oh, no. In the first place, Evvie and I like to do a little sociable drinking in the evening. We took along an extra bag with some bottled goods in it because there's some places down there where you have trouble getting it. But the Bracketts—*they* don't believe in drinking after dinner. They want to hit the sack by ten o'clock and get up and hit the road at daybreak. Cool of the morning, they call it. Well, cool of the morning was made for sleeping, in my book. You ask me, that Freddie Brackett's nothing more than a big goofy farmer at heart. Who wants to spend their vacation getting up at the crack of dawn? Well, we didn't, so we just did things the way we like to do them. We'd be in a hotel and we'd sleep till, say, eight o'clock, and then we'd take our time getting dressed, and go down to get breakfast, and there they'd be—sitting in the lobby, tapping their feet, all set to go, bags packed and in the car. They'd say that *they'd* had breakfast an hour and a half ago, and they'd smile and make some crack about the night club set. They'd let on that they really weren't miffed about it, but I could tell they'd enjoy seeing us stretched in our graves."

"I don't think," said Evvie, "that they really got too upset about that. After all, you've got to take into account the habits of the people you're traveling with. The thing that griped me was the way Freddie Brackett threw *our* money around. Tips! You wouldn't believe it. He's certainly got a lot of the show-off in him. And I happen to know that he and Marge don't *have* money to throw around. I just simply had to put my foot down about it."

"I think I know why Freddie leaves big tips," said Pudge. "It's to make up for Marge and her damnfool actions in a restaurant. If I were a waiter I'd walk in and dump a bucket of hot soup right over her head. She can't make up her mind what she wants. Everybody else has ordered long ago, and Marge sits there and taps her teeth with her fingernails and hems and haws and asks fool questions. Maddening. Absolutely maddening. Then when she finally does make up her mind, and gets exactly what she ordered, about half the time she takes a bite and then yells for the waiter and tells him it's not cooked enough or it's cooked too much or the sauce is clabbered, and so she makes him take it back and then she goes through the whole operation again, ordering something else. If my wife behaved that way I swear I'd keep her home and make her eat out of a trough. Great day in the mawnin' ! "

There were a few moments in which nobody said anything. Then I remarked that it sounded like a real lively trip. "One thing I'll bet," I said to Pudge, "is that you kept 'em laughing all the way."

He glowered. "Look," he said, "I don't mean to brag, but all the people I know seem to think I'm pretty handy with a quip. But if you want to know what happened, I'll tell you. Freddie Brackett had the unmitigated gall to tell me I was making a fool out of myself. *Him!* You must know about *his* sense of humor."

"He twists up factory signs," said Evvie.

"How do you mean?" I asked.

"Oh, it's a little thing he's been doing for years," said Pudge. "He's always looking for signs on factories and stores and he twists the meaning of them."

"We used to think it was a scream," said Evvie, "because he was satisfied to twist up just one or two signs."

"But this trip," said Pudge, "he nearly drove me out of my mind. All day long he kept it up—hours and hours and hours."

I said it still wasn't clear in my mind what Freddie did in the way of twisting up signs and they were able to remember a few examples. Freddie would see a sign that said HACKENSCHMIDT TANNING COMPANY and he'd say, "That's where they tan hackenschmidts." Or the sign would say, ACME INCINERATOR. So he'd say, "All the people in that place are busy incinerating acmes." If he saw NATWICK FURNISHING COMPANY, he'd say that was where people went to get their natwicks furnished. They'd pass a sign, FINNEGAN LAUNDRY, and he'd say, "Let's stop here. It's been weeks since I had my finnegan washed and ironed." He'd watch for a thing like HORNBOSTEL MANUFACTURING COMPANY and remark that this was the only place in the United States where hornbostels were manufactured.

"I don't mind a guy trying to be funny, cheer everybody up," said Pudge, "but this guy Brackett *saturates* you with the same line of stuff, all day long, day after day, no change of pace. There were actually times when I felt like getting out of that car and catching a plane for home."

"Now Pudge," cautioned Evvie, "we agreed we weren't going to dwell on those things. What's done is done. I think we ought to forget about it and just write it off to experience."

"Evvie's right," I said. "The best thing to do is just

forget about it." I got up to go and they walked out to the driveway with me.

"Nice of you to stop by," said Evvie as I got into my car.

"Yeh," said Pudge. "Why don't you folks drop around more often? We don't see nearly enough of you, considering we're neighbors."

"Say!" exclaimed Evvie, "that gives me an idea. Why don't you come over next Friday night for dinner? Just the four of us."

I said I'd let her know. And we may even do it. I don't think the McCords will be asking us to go on vacation with them.

A Helpful Architect

May 9–I want to pass along a cardinal principle of the science of house-buying: Have an expert look it over for hidden flaws before you close the deal.

It happened that when I bought my house I knew an architect who lived in these parts, and he agreed to go with me one morning and give the house a thorough inspection. It was quite cold that day and we took a bottle of spirits along in the car.

At the house my expert began his examination in the basement, rapping walls, looking at beams, probing the furnace. After a bit of this we returned to the car and had a swig of spirits, and he said, "Well, so far it looks all right." Back to the basement for more sniffing around for structural defects, and then back to the car for another snifter to ward off the chill, and the architect said, "Good house." Now the first floor, and more wall rapping, and crawling around the floor, and raising and lowering of windows, and then the car and a good stiff drink. "Fine house," he said. "Damn fine little house." Next came the plumbing in the kitchen and upstairs, where there were two baths, then out to the car again, and, "Son, you gotta house here!" Across the breezeway to the annex that would become my office, and my architect was now going about his business with great zest and eagerness, giving off little yelps of joy, and finally we returned to the car and after he had taken a good long pull at the bottle, he turned around and surveyed the premises with eyes that were beginning to glaze a little, and then he announced loudly: "By God, I'm gonna buy 'er myself!"

But he didn'—I did.

On Almanacs and Other Books

May 10—There are few problems in life that cannot be solved through the use of books (like this almanac). If you are clumsy at splicing high-tension wires, there's a book somewhere that will improve your technique. And if love-making strikes you as a pleasant or profitable hobby, there's a mattress manual called Ideal Marriage that will set you to whinnying and, if you're not careful, bounding off through the woods.

One small catalogue of books that we keep in our home requires but a brief run-through to find all the volumes that will teach you the art of rapid reading, how to have enduring passion, the best methods of pickling watermelon rind, how to organize your brains, nerves, and stomach into one smooth-working unit insuring a longer and happier life, the secrets of jujitsu, how to live in Alaska, and the best way of managing the feet in bowling.

In the lists of self-help books there are many volumes dealing with languages, nervous disorders, dog culture, eyesight, and etiquette. I've found books that will teach you to write, to think on your feet, to understand opera without going to it, to be a successful business girl provided you are a girl, to make your child attractive, to run a club meeting under parliamentary rules, sixteen different ways to tell fortunes, to understand electricity, tell jokes, nurse people, have big fun, make bookends, preach a sermon, make and trim your own hats, play cribbage, hang a flag properly, sober up, grow guppies, fix a Diesel engine, spot aircraft, read blueprints, play the piano away from the piano, achieve world peace, measure things, dive, climb a mountain, conjugate French verbs, sue an enemy, run a store, behave yourself in college, recognize snakes, speak Dutch, compute hog prices, recite poetry, hit homers, perform cowboy dances, hitch up a goat, have a baby, act, believe in angels, play the electric organ, make smoke signals, stuff animals, identify common rocks, pitch horseshoes, read palms, and say grace before meals a different way every day in a year.

> The only reason I ever wanted to be tried for
> murder was so I could take the stand and
> say, "At that point everything turned orange."
> –*Sayings of Avery*

Superstitions

[Friday the 13th]

May 13–Looking at the calendar, let us examine the problem
of today–Friday the 13th.

Me, I'm not really superstitious. I take after my father,
who was a rationalist and believed that it is possible to be
superstitious without being superstitious. I was walking with
him once and saw him circle wide around a ladder and I
asked him if it was an act of superstition. "Nawp," he said.
"Not a bit, but I always say it don't pay a man to take
chances." On another occasion I saw him heave a rock at a
black cat, and again I challenged him. "It jist so happens,"
he said, "that I got no use fer black cats."

So whenever Friday the 13th arrives I try to ignore it.
The only recognition I ever intend to give it is to expecto-
rate into the palm of my hand, give the expectoration a
whack with my forefinger, and whichever way the spit
flies, that's the direction I take–searching for a deep, dark
cave to hide in for a while.

Preparing for this day, I've called upon all the magnificent resources of the New York Public Library to furnish

you readers with authentic data, with laboratory-tested signs and portents, as well as do's and don'ts.

If, of course, you are one who scoffs at superstition, you may as well read no further. These premonishments are not for you. Just go on out and bury your fangs in a black cat if you feel that way. Take your buckeyes outdoors and pound them into a mush with a cleft oak sapling if you want to act the fool and acquire a permanent crick in your back. But please try to be tolerant of others. Don't point the finger of scorn at me. Am I to blame if my mother looked too long at a mandrake? (Looking too long at a mandrake is likely to impose idiocy and flat feet on one's offspring. A mandrake is a sonanaceous herb with ovate leaves; there is no such thing as a manduck.)

The books I have consulted contain many matters affecting human conduct on Friday the 13th. We all know people who will not undertake anything in the way of a business transaction on that day; there are others who refuse even to get out of bed. I have heard of a man in Los Angeles who glues an English half-penny over his navel on every Friday the 13th to keep from getting run down and killed by a truck. I think *his* mother looked too long at a mandrake; the only good that'll come of it is that it will prevent him, on that one day, from getting smog in his belly button.

One erudite author, writing on the subject of Friday the 13th, says that if you should encounter a snake on that day, just shout "Garuda!" and it won't bite you. As long as I was already there in the Public Library I decided to go whole hog in the matter of scholarship and so I made an effort to find out the meaning of the word "Garuda." In French there appears to be a slang word, "garouda," which means "to tie up with spurge flax." If I were a snake I think that would give me pause. There is also an Italian word, "garrulo," which if shouted could mean, "You talk too much!" I don't see any use for it with snakes but I'm glad I found it because it will come in handy elsewhere.

℃

If you want to play it smart when a Friday the 13th comes around you should know about the following matters:

Don't turn your mattress on that day; if you do you won't sleep a wink for six nights.

If your cow gets sick on Friday the 13th, which is probable, hang an adder stone around her neck. Use any standard, nationally-advertised brand of adder stone—they're all good.

If you are a baby, just born on this day, have someone quickly bite your fingernails off (unless, of course, you've got teeth already and can do it yourself). If it isn't done, one way or another, you will grow up to be a thief.

Do not throw a peachstone out the window on Friday the 13th. It is a dangerous thing to do, as it might strike a fairy and kill it. (That's what one of the books says.)

If you want to find out the name of the person you are going to marry, Friday the 13th is the time when you should put the white of an eirack's egg in your mouth. Don't swallow it, but keep it there and run out of doors and the first name you hear uttered (unless somebody make vigorous mention of Judas Priest)—that will be it. I spent the better part of an hour trying to find out what an eirack is. An eirack, it turns out, is the same as an earock, and an earock is a pullet. A pullet is a female chicken less than one year old. Bismarck is the capital of North Dakota.

Don't for goodness sake, count your warts on Friday the 13th. That only makes more warts.

If you happen to be a coal miner in England and the other coal miners are forming a union, get them all to assemble around a rock and spit on it. That makes for solidarity, but only in England.

If you are desperately ill, struggle to a window and keep your eye peeled for a comet. If you see one, you can figure on getting well at once. There is nothing on earth that'll cure things as fast as seeing a comet on Friday the 13th.

If you dibble your potatoes on Friday the 13th, your crop will surely fail. And if, on the same day, you pour water on a windowsill, you'll be poverty-stricken all the rest of your life. (I don't know anybody who dibbles potatoes; nor am I acquainted with anybody who goes around pouring water on windowsills. I'm well aware of the fact, however, that it takes all kinds.)

If you are a girl and want to get a look at your future husband, eat a salt herring, bones and all. Then walk backwards to bed, go to sleep, and a fellow will walk into the room with a glass of water in his hand. It will be he. Him. It.

Look around the walls of your home. If you see any pictures of ostriches, take them down and burn them.

If you eat the marrow from the bones of a pig on Friday the 13th, you'll go mad on the first of November. Year not specified.

If you should find it necessary to walk forty miles on Friday the 13th, the thing to do is to get some mugwort and put it in your shoes. Then you can walk forty miles without getting tired. The mugwort has got to be mugwort that was gathered in mid-summer.

If you should see a Malay citizen running amok with a bloody kris, get some peas and start shelling them as fast as you can, and when you come to a pod with nine peas in it, the Malay will fall down dead. Better stay close to a pea field on this one.

If you go hunting on Friday the 13th, you will have

no luck unless you wear a bittern's claw fastened to your coat with a bit of riband. A bit of riband is the same as a bit of ribbon. On the other hand, if a live bittern should fly over your head—make your will. And one additional warning: don't shoot a deer on the mountain of Finchra, which is on the Island of Rum between Oban and Skye, on Friday the 13th. Do it, and you will get the distemper and die.

☺

Most of these matters are on the unpleasant side, but I'm happy to report that there are a few nice things connected with Friday the 13th. Suppose you are afflicted with blackheads. Well, wait till a Friday the 13th, then go out and find yourself a bramble that is shaped like an arch, with both ends rooted in the ground. While the sun is overhead, crawl through the bramble on your hands and knees three times. Your blackheads will disappear. Also your rheumatism and your boils. (The scratches will heal up in a few days.)

Also Friday the 13th is the proper day to drill a hole in a penny. Then so long as you carry that coin in your pocket it will have companions—you will always have money. Provided that you take it out whenever the moon is new and spit on it and then say, "Fetch, penny, fetch, fetch, fetch." And also provided you don't get a mole on the back of your neck, for that means you are going to be hung.

Finally, a word about whooping cough. If you happen to have it today, put out a pan of milk and leave it out until a ferret comes along and laps it. Don't let the ferret lap too much. Just a few laps, then chase him away. Drink the ferret-lapped milk and your whooping cough will go away.

I don't know what the world would do without my kind of scholarship.

Country Quirk

May 20–There is a small phenomenon, part of the country landscape, that perplexes me. A man comes out from the city and pays a small fortune for a country estate. Then he starts spending money improving it, beautifying it, putting in expensive fencing and costly lawns and lovely flower gardens and symmetrical outhouses. Every single detail of his country establishment must be perfect—all but one: he has his name put on his mailbox, or paints it on himself in a scrawl that would get a child expelled from kindergarten.

Avery and the Skywriters

May 21–My neighbor Avery has always been interested in the psychology of the letter carrier who grows weary of his job and in a fit of depression dumps his bag of mail into a sewer. This sort of thing is reported periodically in the newspapers. Avery has been so fascinated by it that it has led him into a bold speculation. Up where we live, planes sometimes appear in the sky and leave great long trails of smoke or vapor. Now and then one of these planes will cross the sky, leaving its trail, then double back and make a parallel line of smoke. Today Avery told me he is convinced that these are sky-writers from New York City cheating on the job. Rather than go through all the intricate maneuvering needed to write their advertising message above the city, they sneak up to North Westchester and dump their smoke, the same way the letter carriers dump their mail.

I've been so busy I haven't even had time to read the warnings on my bottle of Miltown.
–Sayings of Avery

Classified Ad

[Money No Object]

May 28–Today I was reading an article in the new June *McCall's* concerned with the servant problem in America. It said that titled Europeans without any wherewithal are coming over and taking jobs as servants because there is a serious shortage of native Americans who are willing to sign on as hired hands. I am inclined to disagree with the latter half of that statement.

It takes me back to that day, two years ago this month, when I wrote the classified ad. I have four acres that need to be clawed at steadily from spring to late fall. I do some of the clawing myself, but I need a yardman to come in one day a week if I hope to keep the property presentable. The problem has been: where to get the yardman. Over the years I have had several of them. In most cases I've had to go and get them in the morning and then take them home in the afternoon. And not one of them has shown any signs of steadiness and dependability. There have been many weeks when I've had to do all the work myself. It's not so much that I'm lazy—I just like to set loose.

So it came to pass that I was sitting in my office brooding over this problem. Surely, I thought, there must be some way of getting a man who could be depended on, even one who would haul himself to and from work. Then an idea popped into my mind. Why not advertise for one? I'd never tried that.

I sat there and wondered how I would go about wording such an ad. It would have to be composed carefully to fetch the right man. I went over to my typewriter with the intention of experimenting. I wrote the first line as follows:

WANTED–Man to work on premises one day week. Must furnish own transportation.

Pretty good so far. Straightforward and to the point. But then something happened. I continued typing and my classified ad got out of hand. When I finished with it, this is how it read:

WANTED–Man to work on premises one day week. Must furnish own transportation. Weight 180, height, six foot one. Must have good teeth. Ugly. Dress optional. Must know how to cut grass, rake, putty, sodder, start fires, put out fires, rescue people from burning buildings, listen to me talk, mix concrete, prune things, whistle through teeth, fix television set, shovel snow, shovel anything, put up with loud-mouthed guests, invigorate plants, spade, identify the birds, forecast the weather, dig bait, cope with insects, open stuck windows, use telephone, oil seventy motors, name the Presidents in chronological order, kill wasps, name the trees, must be a Giant fan. Must carry folding rule in hip pocket. If carried in side pocket, won't hire. Applicant must be able to distinguish between a bird and a sheep. Kindly get in touch with H. Allen Smith, Old Roaring Brook Road, where the grass is long. Money no object. Will pay $1.50 per hour.

I finished it and read it over and then got out the telephone directory with the idea of making an appointment with a psychiatrist. A few minutes later a relative of mine came into the room and picked it up and started reading it. She said she thought it was amusing and a trifle off-beat. "I think," she said, "you ought to go ahead and put it in the local paper. It'll liven up the classified ad page."

It was published under HELP WANTED, MALE, the following week. The paper came out on a Thursday afternoon and the first phone call arrived at 5:30 P.M. the same day.

From then until after midnight the calls came in steadily, and three applicants arrived by automobile during the evening. At 6:30 the next morning the phone started ringing again and it rang all day and all evening until 2 o'clock the next morning. More people came by car, and some of them were sober. I couldn't sit down to a single meal without jumping up three or four times to answer calls. It went on through Friday, Saturday, Sunday and Monday. By Tuesday it began to slacken off although the calls were still coming at the rate of about one an hour. Long before Tuesday, however, the packing around my nerves began to shred away. Between phone calls and personal visits I tried to consult plane schedules for Australia and Madagascar but I was in such a dither that I couldn't make sense out of anything. The whole project had the quality of a nightmare, so I can't remember all the things the various callers said. Many of them simply said they qualified on all points and earnestly wanted the job. To these I replied wearily that I had already filled the position. One of them gave me an argument and I remember telling him tartly that I had hired a female midget with exceptionally long arms.

The telephone callers employed every known dialect, including Cockney, Italian, Ozark, Greek, Spanish, Seminole Indian, and three varieties of Dutch—high, low, and

Pennsylvania. One call, which got me out of bed at 5 A.M., came from a town in Massachusetts. The operator said it was collect. I asked who it was and heard a man's voice say, "Tell him it's a motor-oiler." I refused to accept it and went back to bed. Three hours later a man called and began a sing-song recital of the names of all the Presidents, including even Chester A. Arthur. Soon after that a young man phoned and said, "I qualify in every respect except as to size. You want somebody who is six foot one. Well, I am one foot six."

In the midst of it all, certain of my friends and neighbors heard about my great travail, and they began dropping in afternoons and evenings. For some reason they seemed to enjoy just sitting and listening to me answer the phone. They said it was more fun than TV. Every time the phone rang they howled with laughter and when I'd demand bitterly, "What's so funny?" they'd simply scream. One of the things I'll never understand is people.

On Tuesday when the pressure was beginning to let up (I was now taking sedatives) a small truck arrived with a Mr. Andrew Fastiggi. He had on a farmer-type straw hat with a Mexican serape draped over his shoulders and he was waving a pennant bearing the word, "GIANTS." He began unloading things from the back of his truck. I stood and watched him, somewhat dazed, and listened to his deadpan monologue. He said he wasn't going to take no for an answer—he wanted the job and he was going to get it because he was a man with get-up-and-go. He dragged out a small stepladder which he said he would stand on in order to make himself six foot one. The serape was for fanning fires that needed to be started, and for smothering fires that needed to be put out. He had a large sheet of cardboard with a crude drawing of a bird and another of a sheep. He unloaded two shovels (one for snow and one for anything), a rake, a sickle, a pruning tool, an electric soldering iron, half a dozen oil cans, a putty knife, a book about birds and flowers, an insect bomb, a telephone directory, a barometer and a toothbrush. He had a folding rule sticking out of his hip pocket and a silly look on his face. While he was unloading all this stuff he talked or whistled through his teeth or recited the names of Presidents. As a climax to the whole proceeding, he took a roll of bills out of his pocket, flung them on the ground, and said, "Money is no object." I was on the verge of telling him to pick up his things and get off my property or I'd shoot him straight between the eyes when I heard the clamor of the telephone inside, and went to answer it. A woman said she wanted the job for her no-good son. She said he was no-good but that at heart he was a fine boy, if someone could only get him off the marijuana. I advised her, in as gentle a tone as I could muster, to take a club and brain him and then go out and hang herself. Then I went up to bed and beat my fists on the pillow like movie actresses do when they are spurned by someone they love.

All bad things come to an end and this one did, and within a couple of weeks my health was restored and I could pick up a cup of coffee without using both hands. I did have a brief relapse when a bill came from the newspaper for fourteen dollars and forty cents. But that wound also healed, and winter came, and then spring, and I didn't even bother to look for a yardman the next year. I just pitched in and did the work myself. I don't think, however, that I'll ever write another classified ad as long as I live. If I lose my bank book, I'm simply going downtown and walk around the streets and ask people if they found it.

> Where there are two conflicting versions of a story the wise course is to believe the one in which people appear at their worst.
>
> *–Sayings of Avery*

Entomology

[My War Against the Bug]

June 5–Right now, just before they come at me again with their fangs bared, I want to speak my mind about insects. The ugly passions aroused last summer have grown dormant during the long cold months, but now that the Season of the Bug is almost at hand once more, I desire to say a few words on behalf of a persecuted minority group, i.e., the human race.

My mind goes back to that rainy day last year when I stopped by the home of a neighbor to borrow a cup of Tanglefoot. I found the lady of the house stalking a fly, swatter poised for the kill. Into the room came her four-year-old son.

"Don't you hit that fly!" he ordered.

I was impressed by his compassion, a quality not often found in four-year-old boys.

"Why don't you want your mama to hit the fly?" I asked.

"Flies is nice," he responded. "They take away all the wotten food."

His mother glowered at him and for a moment I thought she was going to slash at him with the fly swatter. He had, after all, strongly implied that she keeps lots of wotten food around the house. My own irritation went deeper: that child was voicing an attitude that is being hammered at us constantly by the scientists. I'm quite weary of people who urge me to pamper the blacksnake I find in my basement, to be tolerant with bats, to smile encouragement at frogs and toads. If a twelve-foot crocodile came trudging up my driveway, I'm certain there'd be someone right behind him yelling, "Don't hurt 'im! He eats aphids!"

Most of all, I'm fed up with people who insist we shouldn't kill certain insects because they eat other insects. Within the last year, a man in Connecticut urged the public to be considerate toward mosquitoes for the reason that mosquitoes kill birch leaf miners. Even the termite has his advocates, who say that this ugly villain eats up the fallen trees in our wooded areas, thereby contributing to the beauty of the natural world.

Everybody I know, it seems, tells me I shouldn't kill spiders. They do no harm, and they destroy multitudes of pestiferous insects. Leave the spider alone, unless it turns out to be a black widow. It's all right to slaughter a black widow. What I want to know is who's going to turn the spider over for the purpose of looking for the little red hour-glass which identifies the black widow? My ethics may be warped but whenever I see a spider as big as a fried egg I'm inclined to belt him one and ask questions afterward.

Normally I have an ungrudging respect for the scientist, but when he tells me to encourage house centipedes because house centipedes eat lesser varmints, I'm no longer with him. And I have a strong suspicion that he is more frightened of insects than the rest of us. He has taken the long view of the insect situation, and it has unbalanced him a bit.

The long view of the insect situation can be stated briefly. There are more insects on or in the soil of every square mile of the earth's surface than there are people in the whole world. And in addition to those bugs, there are, in the air above each square mile of land, twice as many insects as there are people in the world. These simple statistics are understandable when we consider the fly. One pair of flies sets up housekeeping in April. By August it is possible for them to have 191,010,000,000,000,000,000 descendants, or nearly five trillion tons of flies. This is most disheartening to me. I can remember the day when I killed eight flies in the house and felt as if I had conquered the heavyweight champion of the world.

Those entomologists who do believe in the destruction of certain insects have pursued two courses, both of which are questionable. I was on an airplane traveling to California some years ago and fell into conversation with my seatmate. He seemed to be an amiable and intelligent man and in time I asked him where he was going.

"I'm on my way to Bangkok," he said, "to get some Siamese cisiphuses to kill off the nubby-head whetworms which are devouring the oviposters off all our Jamaica juppernongs."

A few minutes after he made that statement I asked the stewardess to change my seat. By this act I did the man an injustice. Two months later I read about him in the newspapers—he had really gone to Bangkok to get Siamese cisiphuses, and for the purpose stated.

Yet this sort of thing is bad business. Our natural history is crowded with instances in which one pest was imported to destroy another pest with the result that the imported pest became a worse pest than the original pest. The pattern might go like this: a certain bug is eating the leaves off our maple trees. We find out that there is a bird in Europe that eats the bug, so we bring in some of the birds. They multiply, kill off all the maple leaf bugs, and then start slaughtering wrens. So we have to get rid of them. We bring in some Peruvian weasels to destroy the imported birds. The weasels do their job and then begin to annihilate the chicken population of the land, so we import a special brand of poisonous snake from Africa to get rid of the weasels. The snakes turn out to be cat murderers, and something has to be done about them, so we fetch over a boatload of tigers from India and the next thing we know, *we* are all being eaten up. It is a bad system.

The second error of science, and a much more important one, is the Accidental Improvement of the Breed. I'm sure you've heard about it. The scientists developed DDT and other powerful insecticides. For a while, this looked like victory. It happens, however, that the new insecticides merely contributed to the Darwinian theory of natural selection—survival of the fittest. The weaker bugs were killed off, but the bugs with character and stamina survived and prospered. The way I hear it, if a man goes out in a field today and dumps a bushel of DDT on the ground, the insects come flocking in from miles around for a picnic lunch; and having consumed it, they stretch and flex their muscles and growl and then go up and ram holes in the

[75]

man's house (and in the man). The "improved" insecticides, in other words, have produced bigger and stronger and meaner houseflies, horseflies, Japanese beetles, mosquitoes, thrips, lice, and so on.

☺

I have a dozen books about insects and some of them have color plates, showing certain specimens greatly enlarged. If you think the science fiction writers and the comic strip artists, creating their fantastic creatures from outer space, are overly-imaginative, you are wrong. I don't know of any more frightening sight than these color enlargements of common insects. On the day I first looked at the camel cricket, the buffalo treehopper, the harlequin stinkbug, the tomato hornworm, the greenbottle fly, the rhinoceros beetle, the ichneumon fly and the common sheep tick, I decided that this is not a fit world to live in, and I didn't sleep well for five nights. It was wintertime, but I knew those horrible creatures were out there in the ground, pupating or some such thing, and I knew something had to be done about it.

It was conceivable to me that if science, in its efforts to kill off these horrible creatures, had only succeeded in making them stronger and meaner, then it was possible that they were increasing in size and that there might be no reasonable limit to that growth. As things are today, I am not afraid of a Japanese beetle. But if the Japanese beetle gets to be as big as a mud turtle, I'm simply not going to face up to him. I'll take a monster from Mars any day in preference to a tomato hornworm the size of Jackie Gleason.

Yet I think the ultimate solution lies in this very direction. The scientists have not been lacking in application; they only lack imagination. They come up with a great fund of information and then they just sit there and look dumb. I think that I know how we can defeat the insect.

If certain chemical foodstuffs tend to strengthen and enlarge their bodies, then it would seem possible for us to discover chemical methods that would . . . but wait.

Insects have brains. Some have better brains than others. Ants and bees and wasps are able to communicate with one another. There is a certain type of beetle that drills into the lead sheathing that encases telephone cables, thinking he is at work on tough tree limbs. He's being stupid of course, but being stupid is a widely recognized *form of thinking*. Among the many insects that feed on stored grain and flour is a creature called the confused flour beetle. You think he's confused? Not him. He's called the confused flour beetle because he's got people confused—he somehow manages to make people think he is the rust-red flour beetle. Just what he achieves by this is a question I can't answer, but in his own mind he has his reasons. The plum curculio, which attacks various kinds of fruits, is almost as smart as a crow. If someone approaches him and he thinks he is in danger, he plays possum. He drops to the ground, folds his six arms across his chest and pretends that he is dead.

The *Encyclopedia Britannica* says: "The insects . . . lack size and, with lack of size, the possibility of a large elaborately developed brain." By implication then, if he can grow bigger his brain can grow bigger.

An insect's brain, *Britannica* continues, "lacks the many storage cells for memory and the many cross fibres which in large brains permit the comparison of memories which forms the basis of plastic behavior . . . Elaborate instinctive behavior of such higher insects as the ants, bees and wasps indicates that the minute brain is most intricately and elaborately organized. It appears to be the most elabo-

[77]

rately organized bit of matter of its minute size in the world."

Now, here's what we do. Let us discover a method by which we can enlarge the brain of the bug we don't like. Bring him up to a point where he can think. Not too much. Not enough to make him get the idea he wants to run for public office. Just enough so he knows what's happening to him, and so he'll be able to communicate with his fellows.

Then catch him and torture him!

If the Japanese beetles which descend on my flowers and trees and shrubs and vegetables were able to compare memories, and to communicate with one another, I'd have them where I want them. I'd capture one of them. I'd give him a brain-washing he'd never forget. I'd give him the bastinado—a distinct pleasure considering that he has six feet. And I'd invent some new horrors for him. I'd torture him within an inch of his life and then I'd turn him loose. And he'd stagger out to his family and friends and say: "Great day in the morning, boys, let's get out of here!" He'd tell them in his own way all the things I did to him and all the beetles would swiftly depart my premises, never to return. They'd spread the word. They'd all go down to Avery's place and tell Avery's Japanese beetles: "Whatever you do, don't *ever* go near that Smith place as long as you live. Man, that's rugged!"

I'd follow the same procedure, of course, with the flies and the mosquitoes and all the other insects I don't like. I suppose I'd have to tell Avery about it, even though he might get mad and try to put *me* to the torture. If he wants to get rid of his Japanese beetles, it's up to him to do his own torturing, and to pass the word along to his neighbors.

[78]

As in so many other problems, the answer seems to lie in education—education of the insect. If it's made clear to him, even through such a drastic method as pulling out his toenails with red hot pincers, that he is not wanted, he'll go away.

I have read in one of the bug books that the only insect on earth that can turn and look back over his shoulder is the praying mantis. If I have my way, every one of them will be looking over his shoulder at me. While running.

SUMMER

When the picture on my television set starts
to wriggle or flicker, I no longer think it's the
set—I suspect it's me.

—Sayings of Avery

Electronics

[An Intimate Chat with Ed Murrow]

June 10–Somebody telephoned from New York today and
said Ed Murrow wants to do us on Person to Person on June
28th. No pay. Was I interested? Of course I was interested,
but I hesitated. I have been struggling with the notes for a
book, trying to write two magazine articles, and awaiting
the arrival at any moment of Alma Reed, who is coming up
from Mexico to help with a movie story. A lot of things on
my mind, a lot of work piled up, and this Murrow thing
might prove a big distracting headache. It's two and a half
weeks away so I told them I'd like to think it over and that
I'd let them know definitely tomorrow.

June 11–I've decided to do it. The phone went on the fritz
this morning. No dial tone, no operator. I drove two and a
half miles to the village and used a pay phone to call New
York. Told them okay. This afternoon a long telegram from
Ed Murrow. He says he is delighted, looking forward to the
show, "and feel certain you will find this a painless chore
and perhaps even fun." He adds that maybe later on we can

[81]

get together for lunch "and work out whatever few details there may be."

June 12–A green car from the telephone company arrived this morning. A stocky man wearing dark glasses, and a tall, thin, older man carrying binoculars. The stocky man began roaming over the property. I was just starting work, but I left the typewriter and joined him and he asked me which direction was south, and where the Empire State building was. I pointed. "Oh, no," he said. "It couldn't be in that direction." I explained that for ten years the television man had been aiming the antenna in the same direction for the Empire State building. "They gave you a bum deal," he said. "Empire is right over there." He pointed in a direction which I have always thought was the way to Arizona. "If I'd brought my compass," he added, "I'd prove it to you. Damn if I understand how I happened to forget it this morning." I was a little upset, because if this man were right, then the TV installation people have been pointing my antenna at Bermuda. A phone call interrupted us. Somebody at CBS. "There may be a couple of technicians around," he said, "just to check over the situation. Don't let them bother you. Don't pay any attention to them. They know what to do." I went back to the yard. The stocky man had disappeared into the woods. The tall man was in the front yard, peering through the binoculars at the distant landscape. I tried to talk to him but he wouldn't say anything. Just grunted.

June 13–Nelle went to White Plains today. I was in shorts, having lunch, when a station wagon pulled up. Two men got out of it. A short, amiable fellow who identified himself as Chuck Hill proved to be a "remote director." I made a joke—told him I didn't think he was so remote, I thought he was very friendly. The other was a tall, dark man named Bell. Bell is a map-maker and he roamed around sketching the general layout of the house. Hill had a Polaroid camera and took a lot of pictures, indoors and out. I never did finish my lunch because I just *had* to trail them around and find out what they were doing and saying.

I asked them how many people will be here the night of the program. They began counting up. "I figure twenty-two," said Bell. "That's minimum," said Hill. "Say anywhere from twenty to thirty, counting everybody. Not counting you and your family."

"What about food and drink. I've heard you're supposed to have something for the boys when the show is over."

It turns out that this matter is an embarrassment to everybody concerned (except the boys). Mr. Murrow is upset about it—he doesn't feel that people should be put to the additional bother and expense of entertaining the crew. The production bosses are upset because quite often a supply of hard liquor is broken out, and the boys whoop it up a bit, and even sometimes have trouble getting their equipment packed and removed from the premises.

"Almost everybody," said Bell, "will be here early that afternoon, and will be working till around six. Then we'll break, and the crew will go down to the village to eat. After that there'll be camera rehearsal, a walk-through, et cetera, et cetera, and then the show. If you want to have some sandwiches and coffee and maybe some beer that'll be fine."

Just as Hill and Bell were leaving, the telephone man showed up again. The tall bird with the binoculars was still with him. I've concluded that this tall man is not an employee of the telephone company at all. I believe he is the telephone man's brother-in-law, and the telephone man's wife has said, "I wish to God you'd take Joe with you on your romantical motor tours around the lovely Westchester countryside. He's driving me nuts, just standing around here all day staring through those field glasses, looking at nothing, you might say. Take him with you, give him something to look at."

Anyway, he headed for the front yard again, saying nothing, and began staring through the binoculars. The other one wandered around back by the tool shed, and made little explorations into the woods. When I went out he was talking to himself, saying, "We got problems. We got problems." He asked if I would object to their "throwing up a platform" on the back turnaround. I wanted to know what he meant by "platform." He said it was a tower. "We guy it up to these trees around here," he said, "and shoot straight to Empire. I told him to do whatever was necessary. "We got problems," he said, wandering off into the woods.

June 14–It suddenly occurred to me that they're going to shoot down by the pool, so it has to be painted and filled with water. I scurried down and got the paint and in spite of the heat went to work. A long and tiring job. I was resting my back on the terrace when Nelle pecked on the window, pointed toward the front of the house, and mouthed the words, "Some . . . body . . . out . . . there." I circled the house and found a gangling citizen smoking a pipe and looking at the tops of trees. When he saw me he said, "Con Ed. Gotta throw some extra power in here. TV setup. Come over here a minute." I walked with him to the stone wall. He pointed with the stem of his pipe. "Whatta ya think," he said, "if we run 'er in to that pole, let the TV gang take 'er from there?" I don't know why he would ask my opinion—I'm mystified by the functions of a magnetized screwdriver—but I felt flattered and said, "Sounds good to me, but you'd better finalize it with the CBS crowd." "Good idea," he said. "I'll contact 'em." He wasn't sure of our decision, however, for he spent another twenty minutes fretting around the place, staring at things, puffing hard on that pipe. Finally he came to me and asked if he could check something in the basement. I don't know what it was, but he checked it and left.

June 15—Nelle has started worrying about what to feed all those people the night of the show. She remembered that the Henry Wallaces were on the show recently and decided to call Mrs. Wallace and find out what they did. They have an unlisted number so she abandoned that idea. I reminded her that the CBS people said sandwiches, coffee and beer would be okay. But she's a woman and wants more evidence than that. She called Lila, who sometimes cooks for us, and told her all about it. Lila said she helped out the time they did the show from Tallulah's house. She said they had turkeys and hams and all kinds of cold cuts, and potato salad, and olives and pickles and so on. Lila said she'll come and see to it that everyone gets fed. A neighbor lady phoned and spent forty-five minutes talking to Nelle about what she's going to wear. There was no mention of what she's going to *say* on the program; just how she's going to decorate her person. The neighbor lady jollied us up by reporting that she's heard they rip your house to pieces, move every stick of furniture from one room to another, change the pictures on the walls, and take up the carpets and switch them around.

June 16—Finished painting the pool, at last. Nelle has gone out and cut down my two clumps of chives and the sweet basil plants. "They'll look like weeds," she said. This puts me in a horticultural fury but I make an effort to control my temper. Mrs. L——, a woman we met once at a party telephoned. Said she'd heard all about it and wasn't it exciting! Said she has always admired Ed Murrow more than anybody else on TV. She'd just love to drop in the night of the program, just long enough to get to meet him—not to be on the show, of course. I explained to her that Murrow doesn't come to our house—he's in a studio in New York. She seemed shocked to hear this and I don't think she believed me.

June 17–Local paper called. Wanted to know if this is some special occasion, such as publication of a new book. I said it was not. "Well, then," said the reporter, "why are they doing you on the show?" With only mild asperity, I told him that they had run out of people to do, but the sponsor had insisted that they keep going, so they were reduced to using me. "Oh," he said, "I didn't mean it that way. Tell me some of the questions he's going to ask you." I said I didn't know any of them.

June 18–Today the telephone company man was back, without Joe, but with a white-haired companion, executive type. He announced that the "platform" will be erected back of the tool shed. I asked him if he ever found his compass. He said he had, and I wanted to know which way was New York. He pointed. "We can't shoot straight to Empire," he said, "on account of obstruction." I wanted to know the nature of the obstruction. "Rockefeller," he said. "What Rockefeller?" I asked. "Rockefeller property," he said, "down at Pocantico. He humps up between you and Empire. He's about two hundred foot higher than you and gets in your way. So we got to slam up a platform to clear these big trees, throw you across the other side of town to Guard Hill, and bounce you off a reflector to Empire." I wasn't disturbed—I wouldn't have known the difference if he hadn't told me.

June 19–A man from an electrical contracting firm was first to arrive this morning. He has something to do with bringing in that extra power. He wanted to know if my neighbor would object to the wire crossing the corner of his property. I asked him how much of the neighbor's land would be crossed. Just a few feet, at the corner, up in the air, just for a couple of days, then it'd be taken down. "You mean," I said, "that he owns all the air above his property, and could keep you from stringing a wire through it?" He bobbed his head and answered, "Cert'n'y." "Well," I said, "could he keep a plane from flying through his air? I mean, how high up does he own?" He said he 'sposed he owned as high as it goes. "And," I insisted, "he could cause me trouble if I allowed that little old wire to cross his property, just a tiny corner of his property, for two days without getting his permission?" He gave me a long look and then said, "The only reason people own property is to make trouble for people that want to string wires around."

June 20–The question has arisen whether I should play the organ on the show. I said no. An airmail letter from my sister Lou today. She said she never misses the show and is thrilled that we're going to be on it. "I'm sure glad you don't paint," she wrote.

June 21–Another local paper phoned with a lot of questions I couldn't answer. Would Rufus be on the show? I told her Rufus would probably be dead by then—he was out at that moment barking at a transformer switch box on the pole. He spends nine hours a day barking at live enemies, and evenings barking at boxes and trucks. Avery stopped by. Said he's sore about the Murrow program because they never show anybody having a drink. He said I ought to swig at a highball throughout the show, "otherwise you won't look natural."

June 22–Nelle said today that I ought to get out and mow the fields and then fix those two loose bricks by the basement entrance, and maybe cut back the forsythia. When I told her that none of these things will show, she said, "I'm not thinking about TV. Those things need to be done." She was thinking about TV.

June 23–Photographer Bill Warnecke arrived with his wife and two kids. Said he wasn't supposed to come till tomorrow, but the family wanted a Sunday drive. I told him this is practically an unphotographable house because of the topography. The only way to get a decent picture would be from a helicopter. I suggested that if he felt like climbing a tree or two, we could try that. We got out the ladder and went down the hill a bit and he mounted into the trees and began shooting. Later we sat around and reminisced about his father, with whom I worked many assignments.

June 24–Daughter Nancy phoned. Wanted to know if she and her husband Don are expected up here for the show. She said everybody in North Carolina knows about it and expects them to be on it. Told her to come ahead.

June 25–An electrician arrived early this morning, sore as a boil, been over an hour trying to find the place, pretty furious at the human race because of faulty directions. He asked me for a sledge hammer, said he had to ground something. Telephone cars began swishing in and out, then a truck from a Long Island scaffolding company. Two young men began stacking steel frames against the tool shed. I went out and asked them if they would mind being careful about the periwinkle which I've been nursing along on the bank there, trying for three years to get it to spread. One of the men, a rough-looking character, lifted his foot delicately and said, "Oh, sure." As I headed back to the house I heard him say in a highpitched voice, "Don't step on my itty bitty perry finkel! Shees!" The telephone company man, who was sitting on a stone wall, observed this incident, grinned and said, "You think you got trouble now, wait'll Friday. Wait'll *that* gang gets up here! Oh boy!" I sat down beside him and he grinned at me some more and then asked if I were a praying man. "If you are," he said, "you'd better pray it don't rain. We get rain Friday night and you might as well get ready to sell your house. Cheap. We did Arlene Francis up the road last winter, in all that snow and slush and mud, and I think she had to re-do the whole joint, and it was brand new to begin with. She had this beautiful rug, white and gray squares, and in ten minutes you couldn't tell it *had* any squares in it—it looked like the bottom of a swamp." Telephone company cars keep coming and going. Then this afternoon arrived a huge green truck, labeled "Television Program Transmission Service." When it came in view, I half expected the back end to flop down and half a dozen green jeeps to roll out. It was parked in the back turnaround and the driver said, "Mind if we leave this here for the rest of the week?" I said, "Be my guest." A bit later a writer, Dave Moore, and another remote director, Bob Sammon, arrived by Carey Cadillac. They had trouble finding a place to park. There followed a couple of hours of questioning about my personal habits, hobbies and so on. When everybody had departed, I went out and found the tower now risen to sixty or seventy feet. The side door to the big truck was unlocked so I investigated that. It's a traveling laboratory, control room, foundry and factory, with electrical outlets, telephones, instruments boards, tool bins and coils of wire.

June 26–Two men arrived at 7:30 A.M. and began working at the transformer pole. By 9:30 there were fourteen men and four more arrived within the next hour. With them came a Con Edison truck that looks like something Rommel might have used in the desert. Also a telephone company truck with a gay sign, "LOVE my kitchen phone!" Some of the Con Ed men wore orange helmets and two or three put on climbers, which they call their "spikes," and went up the pole or up the big elm tree. A blue steel transformer, about the size of a pickle barrel, was snaked off the truck, swung over the stone wall, and dragged into position half-way up the pole. In the process three little mimosa trees which Nelle had transplanted near the pole vanished as if by spiritistic means. I had told her, time and again, that those mimosas would never grow in this climate. I'm always right about such matters. While this was going on the tower at the back was rising higher and higher. The blond boy was up there, teetering around on the planks, setting the steel frames in place, hollering insults down to his partner on the ground. All over the property there was a clanking and a clanging and a whirring and a shouting and a buzzing, and suddenly I was called to the phone. It was Willard Espy— wanted to know if I'd do a five-minute taped interview for radio. This afternoon a rainstorm came up. The Con Ed operation stopped and I was told that they always cease work when it rains, but the telephone company boys kept going, and so did the tower builders. By now some of these men have become the same as old friends, and I'm tempted to ask them into the house for drinks. Dave Moore called from New York and asked me to measure the windows in my office—he has to bring out a covering to cut down the glare. I asked him if the driveway side of the house will show; if it does, I'll have to trim the trees there. He said it won't show.

June 27—Half a dozen men were already on the job when I got up. The tower acrobat brought a bag of beer and I put it on ice for him. The telephone company man arrived with a photographer, who took pictures of the completed tower. The pictures will be shown to other people who need towers on their property. Everybody vanished for a couple of hours. When they came back I learned that they had been over at the Guard Hill Tower. Trouble has come up. Several men climbed our tower with binoculars and began staring off eastward, yelling about what they could see. There has been a complaint about the Guard Hill Tower— a resident of that neighborhood had gone to the town authorities and demanded to know why the thing had been put up and by whose authority. "The guy is a utilities-hater," I was told. It appears that there are many utilities-haters in the world; they make a sort of hobby out of pestering and harassing telephone and power companies. Because of this particular utilities-hater, a man will have to sleep in his car all night beside the Guard Hill Tower. Later today I drove over there and had a look; the tower was on a re-mote hill, surrounded by woods, and I couldn't see any reason for complaint.

June 28—The big day. Cars were flowing in and out all morning. The real excitement didn't begin, however, until after lunch. Then the CBS people began arriving—automobiles loaded with cameramen, engineers, and other technicians. Remote Director Sammon was one of the first to get here. Around two o'clock a truck bigger than the Chappaqua Public Library came up the hill and consumed almost an hour jockeying into position. It was so big that the men had to go in the woods and cut long poles to hold up the overhead wires for it to pass. Behind it came a smaller truck and now all the men fell to work, unloading coils of cable, boxes of lighting equipment, standards, dollies, cameras and a few hundred other items. The driveway was soon cluttered with all this equipment and Director Sammon called a conference. Briefly he told the camera crews just what the procedure would be. Two cameras were to be set up beside the pool, one in the living room, and two in the office. More and more people were arriving, including Dave Moore, who brought a list of questions which Murrow may ask. Also two men who have the job of moving furniture and after them, two more who are called stage directors. They are the ones who will wave their fingers at us during the actual show.

Around six o'clock half the workmen departed for the village to eat and when they came back, the others went to dinner. Lila arrived and fixed Nelle and me something to eat. Don and Nancy came in from New Jersey. Dark had fallen and there was no way to count up the number of people on the premises—there must have been between thirty and forty. A makeup man arrived and set up shop in the guest room. A young man fitted me with a traveling microphone. I had to put on an undershirt. The mike was pinned to it, with a wire running down my pants leg and with a flat battery in each of my hip pockets. When all this had been installed I put on my black silk shirt which I bought at a fantastic price in Mexico. We had a walk-through for the cameramen and Director Sammon, who functioned from inside the huge truck, called out to me that my shirt was too dark, would I please change to a lighter one? I hurried to my room and dug out a blue one and put it on. I went before the cameras again, and Sammon reported that he was sorry, but the fabric on this one was too heavy, muffled the sound, so I changed again and this time it was okay. There was another walk-through for the benefit of Ed Murrow, with casual conversation between us. Then the makeup man went to work on us. All this while the young man who installed my microphone kept popping up behind me and saying, "Excuse me, Mr. Smith, but could I change your batteries again?" I'd lift my coattails, he'd take out the old batteries and replace them with fresh ones. This happened every twenty minutes and I asked him if that was all he had to do. "We've got to be sure," he said, "that your batteries are good when you go on the air." As program time drew near, the makeup man grabbed me on the back terrace (I was holding still for a final change of batteries) and began spraying my head from a small can. I demanded to know what it was—I suspected it was something to keep moths and other insects from flying around me. "Satin Set," he said. "It's quite windy, and this'll keep your hair from blowing around." "Good God!" I said, and took my place near the totem pole. The program opened with the other people, the Nielsen family in Chicago, and then switched to Mount Kisco. It went off without a hitch. Our part lasted about eleven minutes and I'm told that the impression on the viewer was one of great calm and serenity; people remarked that I certainly had the ideal sort of place for writing—so peaceful, so rustically quiet, so relaxing. The moment it was over all hands moved into the house for food and coffee and beer. Half an hour later the men were at work in the semi-darkness, packing up their equipment. The trucks and cars began rolling away. By one o'clock we were alone, except for an owl that was hooting in the backwoods, and the distant sound of an auto horn on the Saw Mill River Parkway.

Avery's Law of Lubrication

June 29–My neighbor Avery is forever up to some kind of ingenious mechanical adventure. In his basement I have seen a bushel basket half full of inoperative flashlights–he cannot resist taking a flashlight apart and bending little things inside of it so it won't work at all. I walked in on him one afternoon last week to get away from the pre-TV spectacular at my place, and found him with a chicken feather and a bottle of sewing machine oil.

"Oiling up my specs," he said, and went on with the job. He was lubricating the tiny hinges by which the arms of his glasses are attached to the frame.

"Do the hinges squeak?" I wanted to know.

"Not that I've noticed," he said, and then gave me a patronizing look. "Everything," he said, "needs a little oil now and then."

Plumbing

June 30–It is my belief that in the country, at least, toilets are more eccentric than they are in the city. Most of the toilets of my acquaintance can be cured of their eccentric behavior by simple jiggling. The water continues running so you step back into the bathroom and give the flush lever a brisk jiggle and the shameful mechanism somehow adjusts itself. For one period, the toilet in our downstairs powder room would stop operations only after the cold water had been turned on at the nearby basin. We felt that this was a very remarkable toilet, with personality, until the Robinsons came up with one that would not stop until a faucet had been turned on in the kitchen, forty feet away.

However, today a woman who lives on Bedford Road told us about a toilet in the home of her next-door neighbor, a toilet with almost human intelligence. About once every week or so this particular toilet refuses to shut itself off. The people of the house have a way of fixing it. They simply start talking in an offhand way, saying, "I'm going to get on the phone and call the plumber and he'll fix it." And the toilet quickly stops.

If I ever get around to it, I'm going over and make an offer on that toilet. I'd like to have it. Teach it to do tricks. Maybe teach it to chase a ball.

Logic in Arkansas

July 2–Sometimes I get to despairing, and I think that my reason is failing. But then I think of the barber in Arkansas described to me by Norris Goff. One summer day this barber reached a big decision. He marched to the front entrance of his shop and took down the screen door. Naturally people asked him why. "I finely figgered out," he said, "that a screen door jest natcheral atracks flies."

I'm suffering from natural causes—a real bad
condition—more people die from it than from
anything else.

–Sayings of Avery

Fourth of July

[Pop Elwood's Parade]

July 5–It isn't often that I feel like writing an indignant
letter to a newspaper, especially the North Patent *Courier*,
but this item in the *Courier* made me want to take pen in
hand and howl down the wind. Here is how it read:

C. J. ELWOOD
DIES SUDDENLY

Chauncey J. Elwood, 83, retired plumbing and heating contractor, died suddenly Monday night at his
residence on Gorme Street.

Mr. Elwood was a lifelong resident of North
Patent. When he was a young man he founded his
plumbing and heating establishment on South Lengel
Street. About 25 years ago he sold the business to Jack
Vincent, the present owner.

Since his retirement Mr. Elwood had been a
familiar figure along Main Street and at weekly meetings of the Village Board. He is survived by his wife,
Martha.

Funeral services will be held at 10 A.M. Thursday
in the First Presbyterian Church, with burial in Cedar
Grove Cemetery.

Four piddling paragraphs. And not the slightest mention of the parade. The first time I read it, it was inconceivable to me how anyone could write a single line about
Pop Elwood without some reference to that parade. But
then I remembered that the present editor of the *Courier*,
Fergus Bonesteel, has only been in North Patent for three
years and Pop's parade was eight years ago. And I reminded
myself that weekly newspapers can be pretty abrupt in
their obituary notices. A man can live out his whole life
in a small town like North Patent and in the end he gets
maybe three or four routine, formalized paragraphs—less
space than a bungalow burning down. It seems to me
there should have been at least a full column about Pop.

The story of his parade really begins on that soft,
warm May night eight years ago when he walked into the
regular weekly meeting of the Village Board and exchanged
glares with the new mayor. The room was packed and
every seat was taken except one—the third row chair, on the
aisle, which was always kept vacant for Pop Elwood.

He had been occupying that chair week after week
for more years than anybody could remember. He was a
bald-headed little man with a white mustache, spry as a
chickadee, and he was almost always frowning. A lot of
people thought he was comical, and I suppose he was, but
I could never go along with those who said he was more
than a trifle cracked. He was just one of those people who
are born to be *agin* everything.

He was in his seventy-fifth year that May night when
he came down the aisle to take his customary seat and I

remember that he was greeted with a small patter of applause. The new mayor, Henry Cherry, was presiding at his first board meeting and the crowd had turned out, of course, to see just how Pop would handle him. It was certain to be fun, Henry Cherry being a mere kid, with a butch haircut, even though everybody agreed that he was about the smartest young lawyer to come along in many a year. I had a distinct feeling that maybe the voters elected Henry mayor just so they could see Pop Elwood go after him. And there they were: Pop with his frowning eyes fastened on the mayor and the mayor staring back at Pop, as grim and solemn-looking as a Hereford cow. A moment after Pop sat down, there came one of those sudden silences and it lasted just long enough for everyone to hear Virge Belton's half-whispered crack: "Hey, Pop, you gonna rip his didy off?"

There was a wave of laughter over the room, punctuated by the sharp rap of the gavel. The young mayor had heard Virge's remark, but the grim expression never left his face. The meeting came to order and the first five or six minutes were devoted to routine matters and then, quicker than anybody had anticipated, Pop Elwood was on his feet. It was evident from the way he started that Pop was going to make one of his "State of the Village" orations, laying down the law to the new administration, stating his views on every current problem and project from the garbage disposal plant to the new parking lot back of the depot. He was just getting into the swing of it and, for the first time in anybody's memory, was beginning to talk about juvenile delinquency, when he was interrupted.

"Mr. Elwood," said Mayor Cherry, "please excuse me for breaking in like this, but I have something to say to you if you don't mind."

Pop stopped in the middle of a sentence and stared at the mayor. Nobody had ever interrupted him like this before, at least not so early in his speech. He opened his mouth as if to protest, but couldn't seem to find the words, and just stood there while the mayor went on.

"I want you to understand, Mr. Elwood," came the stern voice of Mayor Henry Cherry, "that the people of North Patent have elected me to be their mayor. I'm well aware of the part you have been playing in these meetings down through the years. I know all about you and I have my own personal opinion about your activities. It may be that you contribute a little entertainment to these affairs, but we're not here for a vaudeville show. We're here for a serious purpose, to take care of the village business."

Pop had been standing there, his eyes growing wider as though he couldn't believe what he was hearing. He wasn't real angry yet, but he had to get his oar back in the water before the boat turned over.

"You listen to me," he almost shouted. "I'm here as a taxpayer and I'm gonna see to it you don't pull no funny business." He paused just a moment, glancing quickly around the room, a small grin showing on his face, and then, quickly, he added: "I got private information that this board is gettin' ready to put over a big swindle on the taxpayers— that this board is gettin' ready to appropriate money so's to buy the mayor a new tricycle to ride to work on, and by George I'm not . . ." The rest of the sentence was drowned out by laughter, and then the mayor whammed his gavel.

"In your own mind, Mr. Elwood," the mayor said, "I'm sure you consider yourself to be a statesman of the gadfly variety, dedicated to keeping the village government in line. Well, sir, I'm going to disagree with you. To be perfectly honest about it, I consider you to be an obstructionist of the worst sort. You are a man with a lot of time on your hands, yet you never do a single constructive thing for this village —you just sit on that bench down at The Bend, like you were a minor league Bernard Baruch, and all you do is talk, talk, talk."

"You're gonna hear plenty more of my talkin' before you're through," Pop shouted at him.

"Other people," the mayor said, "get out and work for the community good, but you simply sit around and gripe. You refuse to belong to any of our fine civic groups. You refuse to serve on committees. I can't keep you from coming to these meetings and belly-aching your head off, but I intend to keep you from wasting the time of every man on this board. Now, if you'll please sit down and *keep your big mouth shut*, we'll get on with our business."

Well, sir, it was a sensation. It was almost like somebody telling the Statue of Liberty to sit down and blow out that torch. Pop reacted as if he had been hit on the head with a mallet. He seemed bewildered, and stared around at the people sitting near him, as if to say, "What hit me?" Then he sank slowly into his chair and lowered his head and looked at the floor a long time. The mayor and the other board members went right on with their business, talking among themselves about the garbage disposal plant. Almost everyone else in the room was looking at Pop. Suddenly they saw his frail shoulders stiffen and his head come up. Once again he got to his feet.

"Mayor," he called out, deliberately leaving off the "Mister" part, "I resent your totaleetarian attitude. For your information I was comin' to these meetin's when you was suckin' your thumb in a go-cart. You got no call to insult me in public like that. I'm a taxpayer and you're my hired hand and I'm your boss."

"You're a taxpayer," the mayor continued, "but that's all. There's a lot more to being a good citizen than just paying taxes. You never *do* anything, Mr. Elwood."

"Don't you dare say I ain't a good citizen," Pop fired

at him. "You talk about all these fool clubs and their fool doin's, and these dumbhead committees and their dumbhead doin's. They don't do a single thing around here that I couldn't do better with one hand tied behind my back."

"I was hoping," said the mayor, "that you would say something like that. Suppose we give you a try. One of the items on the agenda tonight is the matter of the Fourth of July parade. Each year, as you know, the mayor appoints a committee to handle the parade. He also appoints a grand marshal, who serves as chairman of the committee. Now, how would you like to take on the job of grand marshal this year?"

Under normal circumstances Pop would have rejected the challenge, but I could tell he was boiling inside.

"I call your bluff," he said. "Consider me appointed." He stepped into the aisle and turned to leave the room, then faced around again. "Consider me appointed," he said, almost yelling, "and don't bother appointin' no dumbhead committee."

"You can't do it without a committee," said the mayor.

"Don't try to tell me what I can do and what I can't do," said Pop. "I'll do it without a committee or I won't do it a-tall."

"So be it," said the mayor, who was wearing a wry smile by this time. And Pop stalked out of the room.

When he got home that night Martha was looking at television with Sarah Dubley from next door. Pop expected no sympathy from his wife—Martha had been laughing at him in his role of village Cicero for years. Sometimes she humored him, but she knew what the mayor and the Village Board had to contend with; Pop's attitude extended into the government of his home where, he believed, nothing was ever done right.

Once inside his own house, even with Sarah Dubley

present, he let himself go, storming and ranting against "that twerp with the lawnmower haircut" and in the course of his blistering tirade the two women learned that he was going to mastermind the Fourth of July parade, single-handedly. Martha laughed so hard she got a choking spell. When she was able to talk, she said, "I always knew you'd stick your fool neck out too far, and now you've done it. Maybe you don't know it, but you've been booby-trapped. You better get on that phone and back out of this deal right now. You don't know any more about running a parade than the man in the moon. You'll foul it up, and you know it." She turned to Sarah. "I predict," she said, "that when this thing is over we'll have to move to some other town."

Pop drew himself up to his full five-feet-three and declaimed: "Course I didn't expect no encouragement and no help from you. I didn't expect none and I don't need none." And he grumped off to bed.

☾

Pop began deviating from his normal routine the next morning. For years it had been his custom to leave the house at 8:10 A.M. so he'd be at the depot in time to see the 8:16 pull in. After that he had coffee at Bobo's Diner, and then he proceeded to Blalock's Hardware Store where he spent the next hour gassing about affairs local, national and international, but mostly local. From Blalock's, when the weather was nice, he moved on to the bench at the corner of Main and Jefferson.

There is an unusual sort of Main Street in North Patent. It consists of North Main and West Main. The point where the street curves sharply is called The Bend, and that's the center of the business area. Traffic is usually pretty heavy at The Bend, even though almost all through traffic bypasses the village on the superhighway out east of town. Pop's bench was right in the middle of things and he sat there all morning, talking to anybody who would listen, including any stranger who might come along. He spent most of his afternoons in the same spot. He was almost as solid a fixture as the square brick front of the North Patent National Bank across the street. Consequently he was, as the *Courier* put it, a familiar figure to every man, woman, child and dog in North Patent, not to mention people from the surrounding countryside.

On the morning when he began organizing the parade Pop didn't meet the 8:16 train and he didn't go to Bobo's Diner or to Blalock's. He went straight to Artie Vidmer's stationery store where he bought some sheets of drawing paper, a box of thumb tacks, and a card index file. Then he went home where he worked all morning over some mysterious charts, stopping now and then to make a telephone call.

In the ensuing weeks Pop spent no more than an hour or two a day on his bench. He was on the move almost constantly. He'd be seen at one or the other of our volunteer fire houses, or down at the *Courier* office, or going from store to store and from office to office in The Bend, calling on merchants, professional men, school teachers, clergymen, clerks and mechanics. One day he was over at the hospital arguing with Doc Porter, the superintendent. Doc Porter said later that Pop wanted him to put all the patients in wheel chairs and have the doctors and nurses push them in the parade.

☺

One afternoon I found him on his bench and stopped to ask him how he was making out. I always got along well with Pop, probably because I pretended to agree with all his ideas. He said things were going along as well as could be expected.

"I'm gonna give prizes," he said. "It'll be in the *Courier* this week. At first I had the idea of givin' cash prizes, then I happened to think that people would ruther win a twelve dollar cup than a hundred dollar bond. So I've ordered two hundred dollars worth of cups, money out of my own pocket. They ain't silver, but brass with copper platin', and they'll all be engraved with the name of the winners. There'll be one for each division, but most of them go to the kids. And no kid can win a cup, 'less his parents is marchin' somewhere in the parade."

He was all full of schemes and stratagems but mostly he was depending on his persuasiveness as a talker. By mid-June people all over town were chattering about Pop's parade, grinning about it, actually making fun of it. At the same time, however, there seemed to be an underlying senti-ment in his favor. People were laughing at the way Pop was scurrying around town, but they were also offering him their cooperation—maybe to get him off their necks. Take Charlie Blaine, for example. Charlie runs the laundry at the lower end of Jefferson Street.

"Pop's been in to see me three times already," Charlie said. "But he's been in to see the girls and my drivers half a dozen times. This town has never had a parade with floats in it, far as I can remember, but Pop's talked my people into fixing up a float all full of soapsuds."

During the final two weeks Pop seemed to step up his activities and, at the same time, he grew secretive about his plans. If anybody asked him how his parade was coming along, he'd just shrug. There were reports that he and his wife were not speaking to each other and that Martha was threatening to put their house up for sale. Nobody knew quite what to expect.

❧

The parade was scheduled to start moving at 10 A.M. on the Fourth. It turned out to be an overcast day but the radio didn't say anything about rain. As in the past the units were to form on West Main and about half past eight I drove downtown to watch the fun. When I got to West Main I was surprised to see that the parade was already lined up. There were eight floats—nothing that would take any prizes at the Tournament of Roses but pretty fair for a town our size. The high school band was just moving into position out near Binford Street. There was one division of about fifty boys and girls with bicycles, and another with smaller girls pushing doll carriages. Behind the doll carriages was a group of twenty or thirty kids with soapbox scooters, and a gang of youngsters on tricycles. Suddenly I noticed that even though the parade seemed ready to go, an hour and a half before starting time, people were streaming in from all directions. And Pop was scampering back and fourth along the line, issuing orders. The sidewalks were jammed with a confusion of people, young and old, trying to find their places or, as in my case, just watching.

After a while the American Legion arrived, with their Auxiliary and their fife and drum corps, and then the Lions Club began to form up, and along came Editor Bonesteel with his whole staff, printers and pressmen and delivery boys and all. About this time I discovered that Pop had some helpers—one troop of Boy Scouts. Each boy had a sheet of paper showing the formation of the parade and some of them were threading along the sidewalks, showing people

[105]

where to go. One scout, I think it was Milt King's boy, came up to me.

"Which section you marching in," he wanted to know.

"Oh, I'm not marching," I said.

"We got a division called 'Citizens Generly,'" he said. "Why don't you march with them?"

I said I was willing.

"Well, come on," he said, and grabbing me by the arm he led me down the street about a block and a half and there, sure enough, were the Citizens Generly. What the hell, I thought, and started to get in line just as Pop Elwood came charging down on me.

"Hey," he said, "what you doin' back here? I got you down to drive the front car."

"What front car?"

"The lead car," he said, "up at the head of the line. It's already up there. Big convertible. The boys from the Westchester Garage brought it over but they don't wanna drive it—they're marchin' in their own unit and wanna make a good showin'."

"Who'll be in the car?" I wanted to know.

Pop gave me a wry look. "Who else," he said, "but the twerp."

I started walking toward the front of the column—past Sunday school groups and fire engines and the Knights of Columbus. I glanced back westward and as far as I could see there were paraders. I got to the lead car just as Mayor Cherry and his wife arrived. Henry stepped off to one side and peered down the line.

"Well," he said, "I must say it looks like we've got a parade that's a parade. I never dreamed the old man would . . ."

The high school band broke into *Stars and Stripes Forever* and Pop Elwood came hurrying along the column just as our two motorcycle cops took their places in front of the lead car. Pop came up to Henry Cherry.

"Mr. Mayor," he said, "I think we're about ready to start." He took a final glance around just in time to see a young woman come out of a nearby house, a baby in her arms, and sit down on the front steps. Pop dashed over to her, pointed excitedly down the line, and helped her get a carriage off the porch. She put the baby in the carriage and hurried off to find a place in line. Then Pop came back to the car.

He glanced at his watch. "Time to move," he said.

"Wait a minute, Mr. Elwood," said Henry Cherry. "I want to say a word of compliment to you. From what I can see, this is the biggest parade we've ever had. You've done a magnificent job. I want to apologize to you, right here in public, and I want you to climb in this car and ride with me and Mrs. Cherry."

Pop hesitated a long minute. Then he looked at Henry and grinned, and got into the car. The motorcycles roared and sputtered and started off, and I set the car in motion. We were only a couple of hundred feet from The Bend and in a few moments we were swinging around the curve and entering North Main.

I guess I must have been concentrating on the beauty of the big convertible because I didn't notice anything wrong, but suddenly I heard Pop exclaim: "Good Lord!" I glanced back and saw that he was standing up in the car and staring straight ahead, up the long stretch of North Main, his features working as if he were in some sort of pain. I looked where he was looking, and then I got it.

There wasn't a single human being in sight.

"Great God!" came from the mayor. "Mr. Elwood,

you've got every last person in North Patent marching in your parade and there's nobody left to look at it. I never heard of such a thing in all my life."

"But, but . . ." Pop seemed to be on the verge of weeping. "But you can't *have* a parade without somebody to look at it!"

We were still moving slowly along and back of us was the noise of the band and the fife and drum corps and occasional bursts of cheering from the younger marchers.

"It appears," said the mayor, "that that's what you've got. A completely magnificent parade and nobody to see it."

"But where," said Pop, who was sitting down now, "where's all the people from the other towns around here? Seems to me they ought to be over here to see it, and them that live in the country."

At that moment two nondescript dogs trotted into the empty street about half a block ahead of us. They stopped, turned and looked at the approaching column, then ambled off and disappeared between two houses.

"I can answer that," said the mayor. "The other towns around here heard about your parade, and got the fever, and they are all having their own little parades."

Pop was sitting there beside Mrs. Cherry with his head drooping. He had never even imagined that he would organize his parade so well that he'd use up all the people in town. He was crushed.

All of a sudden my eye caught a flicker of color up ahead.

"Hey!" I called out. "What's that up in front of the Corwin place?"

We could see it a little better as we moved along—it was something red and it was flashing up and down. And then as we came closer, we saw what it was.

Standing in solitary grandeur on the curb was Martha Elwood, and she was waving a small American flag. As we came abreast of her, Pop stood up and bowed low in her direction, and she responded by wagging the flag faster and calling out in her thin voice, "Hoo-ray!"

She was the only person who saw Pop's parade, but she was enough.

———◆———

Horticulture

July 16–When it came time to plant corn this spring I put in half a dozen hills for a starter, digging holes about a foot deep and loading them with commerical fertilizer, and then some soil on top of that, and then the seed. I was squatting there in the garden, patting the soil over the seed, and I got to thinking about the antiquity of maize, and its connection with the Indians, and then I remembered that business they used to teach us in school—how the Indians stuck a fish in each hill. If it worked for the Indians, why wouldn't it work for me? I ceased operations and started for the car with the notion of driving down to Gristede's and buying three or four filets of sole, or whatever fish might be available. Then I remembered that when we had the cats my wife used to buy canned mackerel for them, so I went to the basement and poked around and found two cans left over. I went out and dug two more holes, and opened the cans, and dumped the fish—soup and all—into the holes, and covered it with soil, and put in the seed, and then covered the seed.

At this moment I'm inclined to say that the Indian method works. The corn that was fertilized with canned mackerel appears to be outstripping the corn that was planted with commercial fertilizer. The mackerel costs only thirty-seven cents a can.

I don't care what the books say—I won't drink
wine at room temperature.
–Sayings of Avery

Culinary Matters

[Hambone in the Kitchen]

July 18–An independent survey just concluded this morning shows that among the varied contents of my house there
are twenty-three cookbooks. Most of these volumes carry
affectionate dedications and in every instance, save one, the
dedicatees are female. *The Joy of Cooking*, for example, is
dedicated to a lady named Hartrich; Fannie Farmer's manual
is inscribed to a Mrs. Sewall; Sou Chan's cookbook is dedicated to his mother in Hong Kong, and *Alice Foote Mac-
Dougall's Cook Book* is not quite so exclusive as it's dedicated to all the women everywhere.

Included with the twenty-three, however, is one bright
and shining volume, the *Farmers Market Cookbook* by Neill
and Fred Beck, and it is dedicated as follows:

> To H. Allen Smith
> –an amiable man of good heart and sound digestion
> who, one time, declined money in token payment for
> an invaluable service rendered the Farmers Market,
> accepting instead a cabinet of culinary herbs.

Now, as one of the few men in all history to whom a cookbook has been dedicated, I feel that the people of this country might be interested in my views on the culinary art. In the first place, my approach to the cookstove is largely philosophical. I attach, for example, great importance to the matter of preparing eggs for cooking. By "preparing" I mean breaking them open. You probably recall that the little citizens of Lilliput had, as their major political issue, a quarrel over the proper method for breaking an egg—whether it should be broken at the big end or the little end; wars were fought over this question, costing the lives of eleven thousand persons and at least one emperor.

My own theory about egg breaking is equally solemn. It is my contention that a man's character and personality, his whole approach to life, can be swiftly evaluated from watching him when he . . . just a minute.

She has just entered my workroom. With a dustcloth. She knows this is against the regulations, yet here she is. "Well," she says with affected cheeriness, "what's the poor man's E. B. White putting on paper this bright morning?" It's contrary to the rules, but I say, "I'm trying to do a piece for the almanac about my cooking. Go away."

"Cooking!" she exclaims. "Your cooking!" She throws back her loose-muscled head and laughs. "I hope," she says, "that it's pure comedy, because that's what your cooking is. Let's see what you've written."

"Hit le chemin!" I say, lapsing into French. "You have forgotten that under Article XXVI of the Twopartite Treaty of 1945, signed and ratified, you are to keep your distance whenever I'm engaged in my work. And don't forget, you've already had your say in the Introduction to this book."

"I'm aware of our treaty," she says, "but a treaty

wouldn't be a treaty unless there was someone around to break it. Anyway, it doesn't apply in this case. I hope you wouldn't undertake an essay on cooking without recourse to my opinion and advice."

At this point I should invoke The Hague, or the dog, or a slippery elm club, but owing to certain flaws in my character, I resort to argument. "This essay," I say, "happens to be primarily about cooking by men and secondarily about cooking by me. Now, go away or I'll turn in your electric can opener."

Exeunt Woman and Dustcloth.

Now, let's see. We were on eggs. As I was saying, it is possible for a man to lay bare his whole philosophical make-up by the manner in which he cracks an egg in the kitchen. The smoking skillet stands before him. In his right hand is an egg. At this instant, speaking allegorically, he is facing up to life. If he is a man of mettle, a citizen to be reckoned with, he must reach out and crack that egg on the rounded edge of the stove temerariously. He must perform the act with resolute confidence. He must cow that egg and crack it, convey it to the skillet, deftly open it so that its contents plop gently into the pan, give the shell halves an expert shake, then deposit them swiftly and neatly in the garbage pail. All of this he must do with an aggressive, forceful, audacious and almost precipitate courage, yet without a hint of grimness. There must be no momentary hesitation, no sign of flinching—he must crack that egg as if . . .

Good Lord! Here she is back again! Now what?

"I've just been thinking," she says, "that you'll make a complete fool of yourself if you try to write about cooking without my help. I don't mean to meddle—I just want to be helpful."

So I read her the part about the egg.

"That's a lovely sentiment," she says, "the way you compare egg cracking to life. But you are implying that you crack an egg the way Young Lochinvar or Billy the Kid or Sergeant York would crack it. Tell the truth. Tell about your egg cracking. Tell about the nut bowl."

I think it's altogether extraneous, quite beside the point. Nothing shameful about it, though. It happens that I'm just not built to break eggs. I have the wrong temperament for it. Probably something that happened to me in my dim childhood. I have been striving earnestly for years to crack an egg in the madcap manner. I stand there with the egg in hand, tighten my jaw, tense my muscles, hesitate, wince slightly, and then strike. If I do manage to get it over to the skillet with only a small dribble, then I seem to have trouble getting it open. Perhaps I lose my temper, my thumb crashes through the shell, and stabs the yolk, converting a plan for fried eggs into a plan for scrambled eggs. Fragments of the shell usually drop into the pan—a circumstance that almost drives me crazy. Sometimes, in the tense excitement of the moment, the whole business drops into the pan. I am a man of even disposition, yet there is something maddening about this sort of an accident; on one occasion I kicked the stove and on another I carried the pan outdoors and hurled it and its horrid contents over the hedge and into the woods. I know *how* it should be done, but I sometimes suspect that I have a talent for getting hold of eggs with defective shells; quite often they refuse to crack across the middle as they should, but crack lengthwise because of natural faults in the shell structure. And in these moments of despair (after cursing the whole of henhood) I sometimes think of those people who manage the entire operation with one hand. I have nothing but contempt for them. They are human freaks, close kin to the people who roll their own cigarettes —rank exhibitionists. There is no occasion for . . .

She is still here, hovering over me. "That's not the whole story," she says. "Go on. Write it down. Write about the nut bowl."

"Blankety-blank-blank!" I say. "Haven't I already admitted that I'm not very handy at cracking eggs?"

"The nut bowl," she says.

I don't see that it fits in, but—

Usually it was only a dribble—a thin streak of albumen between the edge of the stove and the skillet, and she didn't object so much to that. What she couldn't tolerate was the total egg, shell and all, failing to reach the skillet, failing even to get started toward the skillet. This happened more times than I care to think about. It's a tragedy directly traceable to my philosophical approach—my knowledge that the cracking of an egg must be done in forthright style, with courage and aplomb. Quite often this philosophical consideration leads me to bang the egg much too forcefully on the edge of the stove and the whole thing escapes from me and runs into the burner apertures or down the side of the stove to the floor. I'll be fair about it—it's quite messy. But I do think she was carrying criticism a little too far when she inflicted the nut bowl on me. It's a wooden bowl which she dug out of the attic and it has a grooved elevation in the center, put there I suppose to hold the nutcracker. She keeps it in the kitchen and I am under orders to use it whenever I attempt to break eggs. I must crack them on the wooden centerpiece; then, if the eggs get away from me, the mess is confined to the bowl.

But enough of eggs. Cooking is not all eggs. As a matter of fact the handling of eggs is, and should be, a woman's prerogative. Where a man shines is with meat. Meat and seasonings. A woman simply doesn't know . . .

"*There's one other thing about eggs,*" she says.

"*I'm finished with eggs.*"

"*What subject are you on now?*"

"*The general theme, if you have to know. I intend to show that men have a natural talent for the more delicate nuances of cooking. Why don't you go away! Go work on that three-million-dollar error in your checkbook.*"

How strange are the mental processes of the female! Their attitude toward the man in the kitchen is obviously one of pure envy. They *know* that men have them backed off the map when it comes to cooking. They *know* that all the great cooks are men, that the various gourmet societies are composed of males who hold solemn conclaves for the purpose of savoring food that has been prepared by other males.

My skill in cookery dates from the acquisition of that cabinet of culinary herbs. Before the gift arrived our kitchen contained an absolute minimum of seasonings; Nelle had some salt and some pepper and some allspice (which she believed was a handy combination of several spices, egad!) and some cloves and a jar of bay leaves that had been around for fifteen years and had turned into leaf mold. As I recall there was some vanilla extract and maybe a couple of other seasonings, such as sage and nutmeg. But no cumin seed, no cardamom, no thyme, no rosemary, no orégano, no basil or borage, no marjoram and not a seed of lovage. We now have thirty varieties of herbs and spices, but the lady of the house scorns to use anything but salt, pepper, allspice, vanilla extract and bay-leaf mold. She refers to my spice collection as "clutter" and whenever she's cooking, say a stew, she'll call out to me, "Come on out and put some of that grass seed in the pot if you insist on it." She pretends to hold my herbs in contempt, yet I know that she is secretly entranced, and awed, by all those lovely fragrances. I say she's awed, because she's a little frightened of them.

One morning she complained of an illness which she attributed to something she had eaten. She tried to remember what it was.

"Oh," she suddenly announced, "now I think I know what it was. One of your spices. You spilled some on the kitchen table yesterday afternoon, and I was tasting it. It looked a good deal like chili powder, but it had a strong salty taste. I meant to ask you what it was—it tasted real good."

I went out and checked through the bottles and jars. Nothing there of a reddish, chili color that I had been using. Then I remembered. A big tin can, about quart size. It contained a reddish powder. I had been throwing it on the hot coals in the fireplace. It is a gritty preparation which creates a powerful gas; the gas shoots up the chimney and cleans the flue. She had eaten a tablespoon of this stuff. And she thought it tasted real good!

Wup! Hold everything! Here she comes again. What on earth ever possessed me to undertake a composition on cooking? What kind of a . . .

"I've been thinking," she says, "about how most men are outdoor cooks. They wouldn't go near a kitchen stove, but the minute anyone suggests cooking outdoors, they go into their act; they slap on their ridiculous chef hats and their goofy aprons with wisecracks all over them and they start to work over a bed of smoky coals. What hambones! They've got to make a production out of it, in the cheapest theatrical sense. It's a wonder to me they don't hire a line of chorus girls to prance up and down in front of the barbecue

while they're reducing the meat to cinders. Indoors or out, they ham it up, and a self-respecting buzzard would walk away from their cooking. Just what kind of phony story do you intend telling about your outdoor cooking anyway?"

"I'm going to say that outdoor cooking is all right for the man who's an amateur. Personally, I'm not too strong for it. An outdoor barbecue is first cousin to a picnic, and picnics are for the birds. I'm inclined to be a little contemptuous of the man who never cooks unless he's outdoors—who isn't willing to stand up to the kitchen stove and show his womenfolk . . ."

"You," she says, "are going to tell the truth. Otherwise I write to your publisher and expose you. Go on, write it out. Begin with the goggles."

It's old stuff, ancient history, but I don't mind telling it. A man, at least, has got a little imagination. A man can be practical.

I walked into Fox & Sutherland's store one day and asked Jack Sutherland if he had a cheap pair of goggles. "You riding a motorcycle now?" he wanted to know. "No," I said. "Well, what do you want goggles for?" "For frying chicken," I said. "Oh, I see," he said, and got me a pair.

At that period I not only wore goggles when I fried chicken, I also put on a pair of leather gauntlets and an old felt hat with the brim turned down. This costume was eminently sensible, protecting me from flying grease. For some reason, which I've never been able to explain, every time I tried to cook, things exploded. I don't mean the stove—I mean the stuff I cooked. The minute I put anything on the fire the atoms in it began splitting. At that time I was specializing in Latin American cookery, and the explosive qualities of Latin American dishes are spectacular.

There were times when I stood at the stove in a veritable rain of hot rice.

The subsequent trouble, of course, lay in the fact that my cookery not only exploded all over me, but got on the kitchen floor and sometimes on the walls. My spaghetti sauce (with sweet basil and a whisper of orégano) was delicious, but occasionally, to taste it, you'd have to lick it off the walls.

She was willing to clean my culinary delights off the floor (as a matter of fact the dog did most of the job until he got sick), but when it came to the walls she hit the ceiling. At one point she was threatening to go to a local moving company and buy pads—the kind that are used to cover the walls of elevators when furniture is being transported—and hang them around the kitchen on such occasions as I chose to cook. I remember that one winter day I decided to undertake a suckling pig. Exploding a pig was more than she could bear to think about. She checked over the insurance policies and said I couldn't do it—we weren't protected. Well, as you know, marriage consists of a series of compromises—I didn't cook the pig. She did, though, and out of the goodness of her heart let me explode the apple.

"Oh," she says, "aren't we being funny! Why don't you get down to cases? Get to the big point—the new kitchen."

Well, we got a new kitchen. About a year ago we had the whole thing modernized. And when the job was all finished she issued her manifesto. I was exiled from the kitchen. Me! To whom a cookbook is dedicated!

That's the real reason why I do my cooking nowadays at the outdoor fireplace. I suffer no searing ignominy from it. I can perform wonders on that outdoor grill. I still endure explosions, but they don't seem to be as severe as in the old days, and they hurt nothing but the trees. And in spite of a certain humiliation that goes with it, I get a good deal of personal satisfaction out of one fact. In *her* new kitchen the spice cabinet occupies a prominent position on the wall—the only piece of equipment held over from the old regime. And sometimes when visitors come and she lures them in to show off her sparkling new kitchen, she waits until they spot the cabinet—which they always do—and then I hear her say in the most casual manner:

"Oh, yes. That's my spice cabinet. I simply wouldn't be without it."

What a hambone!

Fijian Fan Mail

July 19–I once wrote a dissertation on outdoor cookery which was published in the *Saturday Evening Post*. The mail I got from readers was voluminous and challenging; most of the letters were from men, accusing me of being abysmally ignorant in matters of alfresco cookery. Then, after the passage of three or four months, a letter came bearing a Fiji Islands postmark.

When I opened it, my first glance showed me that it was concerned with outdoor cookery. Without reading further I let it drop into my lap and gave free rein to a weird notion that had entered my mind. Here, I thought, was perhaps the very ultimate in fan mail—a letter from a cannibal. I already knew that for centuries it has been the custom among cannibals to cook outdoors. It has been a further custom among them to *boil* their meat, using large iron pots. At least all the cartoons have always shown it that way. Now, with the unread letter in front of me, I suspected that my cannibal correspondent was eager for technical information about the latest in charcoal grills. Civilized ways had at last, no doubt, penetrated to the cannibal lands and now they were interested in marinades and garlic butter for basting. In short, they have now advanced to the point where they want to barbecue their . . . well, their meat. They may even have learned that food loses vitamins in the process of boiling.

I was, to be frank about it, a little disappointed when the letter turned out to be from an Englishwoman vacationing in the Fiji Islands, asking for recipes best suited to the charcoal grill.

Avery's Biography

July 30–Avery's biography could be written around the number of incidents in which metal or wood or fiber or plastic have viciously turned on him with murderous intent. This week he has been laid up with his sacroiliac substructure painfully out of plumb, and he blames his misfortune on a potato. He was walking along his driveway, bringing the mail in from the road, when he saw the potato. It was lying in the middle of the driveway. He stood and looked at it a while, speculating on the meaning of its presence. It never occurred to him that it had popped off a grocery truck. "Somebody," he surmised, "has been throwing potatoes around here." He stooped over to pick it up and something snapped midway between his hip pockets. He's been in bed for ten days with a wooden door under his mattress, and in speaking of that malicious potato, he is borrowing liberally from the works of John Steinbeck.

Honeysuckle acts just like a child. It's sweet
and good and nice to have around, but if you
don't control it, it will take over and make
your whole life miserable.

–Sayings of Avery

Gossip

[Randy and the Big Smart Alec]

August 8–This afternoon I won back a friend, Randy
Reese, who has kept me informed about goings-on in the
neighborhood for the past three summers. In fact, I still
remember the first day he came up the hill, and the pleasure
I took in his coming. It was an afternoon in early July.
My office is across a breezeway from the house and I was
at work composing a bit of perishable prose when I heard
a light knock at the screen door. He was standing there
with those big gray-blue eyes and he was breathing hard
because he had walked his bicycle up the steep driveway.

At first I thought he was one of those kids who come
around selling tickets for the Scouts or the Boys Club. As
it turned out his call was purely social. I walked back to my
desk and sat down facing the typewriter. He followed me
in and took a position across from me. He was just tall
enough to permit his elbows to rest on the desk, and he was
wearing a smile that seemed to say, "Well, here I am!"

"So," I finally said, "who are *you?*"

"Randy."

"Randy what?"

"Randy Reese. I got the same name as Peewee Reese. Peewee Reese is one of the best baseball players they is. The Mapeses got a new baby last night. Mrs. Mapes is prednant."

There appeared to be an anachronism residing in those last two sentences but I let it go, assuming that somebody had told this boy about the bees and the birds, rather than the birds and the bees. The Mapeses live about a quarter of a mile to the north of me but I hadn't heard about their new baby. And now I was getting this boy identified—the Reeses had been to my house and I had been to their house and I knew they had a couple of children, but I had never been aware of the existence of this Randy.

"Was it a boy or a girl?" I asked him.

"Girl. Seven and a quarter pounds. I saw a snake in Mr. Watson's garden. It was almost three feet long. I told Mr. Watson and he killed it with his rake."

"What kind of a . . ." I began.

"We got a new conmertible," he hurried on. "We traded in that old station wagon and got a new conmertible. It's red. All you do is pull on the thing and the top goes down and then if you want to put it back up if it rains you push on the thing and it goes back up." He paused for a moment to let this splendid news have its desired effect. Then he said: "Why did the moron tiptoe past the medicine chest?"

"I don't know," I confessed. "Why?"

"So he wouldn't wake up the sleeping pills."

I laughed, but he didn't; he just stood there and grinned. Up to this point I had been hoping that he'd terminate his social call and let me get back to work, but now I was beginning to enjoy him. I stood up.

"Right now," I said, "I've got to go out and do some chores."

"I'll go with you," he said. "Why is the cook mean?"

"Why?"

"Because she beats the egg and whips the cream."

He trailed along after me, carrying one of the wastebaskets for me when I went to the incinerator to burn some junk mail. He wasn't exactly a chatterbox—he didn't talk *all* the time. But when he did talk it was usually news and gossip about people who live on our road, or it was another moron joke. I was to find out later that Randy spent hours bicycling over the neighborhood, calling on people just as he was now calling on me. He absorbed everything he saw and heard, and he knew more fresh and lively gossip than any of the ladies on the road. Oscar Wilde said that history is merely gossip; I go him one better and say that gossip is merely history.

About twice a week for the remainder of that summer Randy came up the hill. I remember that about the second or third time he called I was typing, and I continued until I'd finished off the page.

"Is that the only typer you got?" he wanted to know.

"It's the only one," I said.

"My Daddy," he said, "has got a hundred typers. I mean a thousand. Mrs. Munson is on a dite. She don't eat anything but celery and soup. Mrs. Porter said Mrs. Munson wants to get skinny and look young."

I didn't pay much attention to the news of Cora Munson's diet; I was trying to unscramble that statement about the thousand typewriters . . . I mean typers. I asked him where his Daddy kept his thousand typers.

"Down to his office in the city," he said. "He's got a thousand typers and a lady to go with every one. Have you got a spoon?"

"We've got a thousand spoons," I said.

"If you take a spoon that's real shiny and look in it, you'll be upside down," he informed me. I was digesting this intelligence when he asked me why the moron took the ladder to the party. I didn't know, so he told me, "Because the drinks were on the house." After that we went out to perform some more chores.

℀

About the middle of the summer my wife began to grow slightly disturbed over Randy's visits. She had a feeling that he was interfering with my work and that, in consequence, my bank balance might suffer.

"That boy," I told her, "is one of the most stimulating kids I've ever met in my life. *He'll* never be a juvenile delinquent. There's not a shred of rebellion in his makeup. He has a genuine love for people, and I enjoy having him around."

And so he continued coming. I do quite a bit of outdoor work around my place and fancy myself as a fair sort of handyman. On those days when Randy came he'd follow me around like a puppy. He always watched whatever I was doing with close attention and he always kept the conversation rolling, often with moron jokes. He said that when the moron was dying, he moved into the living room. The moron cut off his arms so he could wear a sleeveless sweater. The moron put his father in the icebox so he'd have cold pop. The moron set the church on fire so he could see holy smoke.

Then came September and I saw him no more, for he

[124]

was back in school. I must say I missed him for a while but by the following spring he was out of my mind. And then he was standing across the desk again, an inch or so taller, a year older, but with the same steady eyes and the same friendly smile. I braced myself for a whole new crop of moron jokes, but I never heard another one pass his lips.

He pursued the same routine all summer, calling after lunch about twice a week. He trailed me around the premises and watched me at work with hammer and screwdriver and paintbrush and trowel. He brought news of all the neighbors. Mr. Watson got a ticket for going through a red light on the Bedford Road and was so mad he said he was going to move to Connecticut. The Kirks had decided to have their vacation in Mexico instead of Hawaii. "It don't cost as much to go to Mexico like it does to Hawaii," Randy explained. Mr. Stevens had a poker party that lasted nearly all night. There were six men at the party and they drank seventy-four cans of beer (Randy had counted the empties). Mrs. Munson had a "puncher" on the Millwood Road and changed it herself. The Congdens were having a lot of trouble with their "seppitick tank."

Soon enough I found that a new conversational device had succeeded the moron joke. Somewhere, probably from a book, Randy had accumulated a series of hypothetical confusions which gave him something to talk about when he wasn't purveying neighborhood gossip. As I recall, he started off with the classical question, "Which came first, the chicken or the egg?" This sort of problem usually throws me into a brain panic, but Randy could talk incomprehensibly for several minutes on the matter of precedence among chickens and eggs.

I'd be out laying a fire in the barbecue and he'd stand

by, watching every move I made but keeping the conversation alive.

"Did you know," he'd say, "that Millie Vollmer went on a TV quiz show and won five hundred and eighty-six dollars and she's going to use the money to buy dresses to get married in to a soldier that lives in Sinnecktady?"

"No," I'd say. "Hadn't heard a word about it."

"It's true," he'd assure me. "I got one for you. If a tree falls down in the forest with nobody there to listen to it, does it make any sound?"

"No," I'd say. "I mean yes." As the summer wore on he came up with more of them. Does a horse push a wagon or does he pull it? Is a zebra a dark animal with light stripes or a light animal with dark stripes? What do mosquitoes eat when there aren't any people?

"That Randy," I told my wife, "is probably the sharpest boy in Westchester County. I mean for his age. He's going places, that kid. He has a scientific sort of mind. He's always inquiring into things, always curious about everything."

"I hope," she observed, "that if he thinks he's learning anything from you, he double-checks it somewhere else."

So we went through the second summer, and again with the coming of autumn the Randy visits ceased.

☻

And now we come to the present year. I hadn't put him out of my mind during the past winter. I'd thought about him often and when April came I actually began worrying over whether he'd take up the old routine. Sooner or later, I thought, a boy as smart as Randy would develop other interests. He was now nine, or perhaps ten, and probably getting involved with things like jet propulsion and nuclear fission. Maybe even girls.

But he came back, and ahead of schedule. It seemed to me that he had grown half a foot since the last time I'd seen him. He came into my office one Saturday afternoon in the middle of May and the first thing he did was ask me if we'd had much trouble with ice and snow on the driveway during the winter. I said that we always had such trouble. "You ought to put some calcium chloride on it," he said. I should have known right then that trouble was coming.

That first day he demonstrated that he had not given up the job of playing gossip columnist for the neighborhood. He was still making the rounds on his bike and apparently other people enjoyed his visits as much as I did. He reported that Mr. Avery was trying to build an outdoor fireplace all by himself. Mr. Avery had dropped a rock on his foot and broken his big toe. Randy had been present and said that Mr. Avery "cursed loud" and that he cursed the rock and the outdoor fireplace and his whole property and he even cursed his big toe. A squirrel got in Mrs. Cunningham's house while she was in Georgia and ate up all the drapes. The Porters had installed a new hi-fi system that cost seven hundred and twenty-four dollars. It was a Christmas present from Mrs. Porter to Mr. Porter but Mr. Porter said *he* was the one that had to pay for it. Mrs. Munson thought that she was getting a "thyroy condition" so Dr. Wake gave her some miracle drugs and she got a terrible rash on her arms and shoulders and a stiff neck that wouldn't go away, and Mrs. Munson said she was going to sue Dr. Wake for a half a million dollars for "mental angrish."

"You know Mrs. Frederick?" Randy asked me. "She's the worst driver in the United States. My mother says so.

My mother says if you ever see Mrs. Frederick coming you should get clear over in the ditch."

Along toward the middle of the summer I found that a significant change had come over him. He was no longer content to watch me work—he had become critical of my techniques. When I was patching the pool he told me I had too much water mixed with the cement. When I was trying to loosen a stubborn screw on a piece of redwood furniture, he said I should get a monkey wrench and clamp it over the head of the screwdriver to get better leverage; he showed me how to do it and I was a little irritated to find that it worked. While I was transplanting some tomato plants into the garden, he stood beside the fence and criticized the texture of my soil. "You better go down to Young & Halstead's," he said, "and get some humus and spade it in." I think that was the first time I frowned at him, but he didn't appear to notice.

❦

About a week ago, he arrived during an afternoon when I was watching a ball game on television. I invited him in and he sat with me for about half an hour, and then the TV set went on the fritz. We lost the picture but still had the sound. It was a good ball game so I began pounding on the set with my hand and even kicked it a couple of times in an effort to restore the picture. Randy promptly intervened, telling me I shouldn't be so rough with a sensitive instrument. He said it was probably a bad tube and asked me to remove the back panel. When I got the panel off he asked for a pencil with an eraser on the end. He began tapping tubes with the rubber end of the pencil and pretty soon he hit one that produced a clonk-clonk sound in the audio. "There's your trouble," he said. He removed the tube and handed it to me and told me all I had to do was replace it and all would be well. No need to call a service man. For some reason his authoritative manner gave me a slow, steady burn. I put the bad tube in my pocket and told him I had to go down to the village and that I'd be gone for a couple of hours so he might as well hit the road.

That evening I said to my wife: "It's too bad about kids. Never saw it to fail. Perfectly wonderful for a while, and then they reach the show-off stage. That Randy's beginning to get too big for his britches."

The next time he came I was just getting ready to give the lawn a mowing. I was oiling the handmower when he came up and looked at it closely.

"Have you had it sharpened?" he asked.

"No," I said.

He reached down and moved the cutter-shaft back and forth.

"Pete sake!" he exclaimed. "We've got to take up the play in the bearings. It won't cut good if we don't. We need a nail and a screwdriver."

With some reluctance I got the nail and the screwdriver. He put the nail into a hole somewhere near the left wheel and held it there and then with the other hand tightened a screw. He'd stop now and then and move the cutter-shaft back and forth. Finally he said, "That'll do 'er." He straightened up and looked at me and continued, "If I was you I'd get some lapping compound. Spread it right along here and then we'll reverse the pinions and she'll sharpen herself."

Damn smart alec kid! Trying to tell a grown man how he should go about fixing his lawnmower!

"Listen, Randy," I said. "I've got a lot of work to do

today. I wish you'd climb on your bike and go for a ride. Go on. Go take a ride."

He looked at me with wide eyes for what seemed like a full minute. Then without a word he walked over and got his bicycle and started down the hill. He turned once and looked back and for a moment I almost relented. But I let him go. I felt that I had done the right thing. I told my wife that Randy was becoming an insufferable little twerp. "He's developed into one of the worst smart alec kids I've ever seen," I said, "and if there's one thing I can't stand it's a smart alec kid."

"What's eating you?" she demanded. "Has he been outsmarting you? He must have told you that you were putting too much basil in your spaghetti sauce."

"There you go," I said, "leaping to fantastic conclusions."

That evening I was trying to read a book but I didn't seem able to concentrate on it. I went to bed early but I had trouble getting to sleep. I kept seeing his face—the way it was when he turned to look back at me.

Yesterday I was still out of sorts. Grumpy. I fooled around all morning, doing nothing. I was waiting for something. I was waiting for lunch time, when I knew he'd be home. A few minutes after twelve I picked up the phone and dialed the Reese number. Mrs. Reese answered and I asked for Randy.

He answered the phone with a rather solemn hello.

"Hi, Randy!" I almost shouted. "Guess what I've got to do tomorrow afternoon? I've got to chop down an ash tree—that big one right below the stone wall. And listen, Randy—I don't see how on earth I'll be able to do it without your help."

"What time?" he asked, his voice brightening.

"Say about two-thirty. Can you come?"

"Well . . ." he said, and I could tell he was remembering.

"I've got some swell jokes," I told him, "about bopsters."

"Two-thirty," he said. "I'll be there."

I hung up and grinned, and then said aloud to nobody: "Sometimes I can be the biggest smart alec on earth."

Bottom of the Box

August 11–I have been yelling about the strawberries for fifteen years. It started on a day like today—when my wife came home from the grocery with a box of strawberries. Passing through the kitchen, I noticed them, and absently walked over and picked up one or two of them just to look at them, and then I proceeded to empty the whole box, examining the descending layers of berries. I knew, of course, that the berries on top would be the big, ripe, unblemished, juicy ones, and that the runts and lopsided and green and half-rotten ones would occupy the lower levels.

So I said to Nelle, "Did you ever in your life buy a box of strawberries in which the berries underneath were as good, or even better, than the berries on top?" She laughed at me. "There was never," she said, "any such box of strawberries."

"Then," I said, "you and all the other housewives of the nation know it, and accept it?"

"Why, sure."

"Don't you suppose," I went on, "that somewhere in our great republic there is a strawberry grower, a farmer, who is a good Christian, and has a conscience, and tries to be honest

[131]

in his dealings with his fellow men—and puts good strawberries on the bottom?"

"Almost all farmers," Nelle said, "are saints, but you expect too much. It just isn't done. It's been this way as long as I can remember. Everybody knows it."

"And everybody accepts it," I said. "Everybody but me."

And I'm still damn sore about it. To my mind it is fraud, pure and simple, and one of these days I'm going to get up on my hind legs, and organize a great popular movement of protest that will likely find its way into future histories of our country under the heading, "The Great Strawberry Revolt."

> I'm getting tired of fighting vegetation on the
> one hand and busting my butt to befriend it
> on the other. To put it in simple language, I'm
> getting tired of vegetation.
> —*Sayings of Avery*

Field and Stream

[The Pleasures of Big Bug Hunting]

August 29–It was silly of me to try to keep it a secret, I
guess. A thing like that is bound to come out. I used to keep
the gun out of sight when visitors came to the house and
even ducked it under a bush when delivery men drove up
the hill. Yet I have an idea that the tongues are wagging
already, from Greenwich to Ossining. If there is one place
on earth where a man can't enjoy true privacy, it's in the
country.

The reason I am going to tell about it now, at the
beginning of a new hunting season, is that I want it told
truthfully. It happens that a friend of mine, a New York
newspaperman, just telephoned my house this morning. I
was out in back with the gun and my wife summoned me
to the phone.

"Hey," said my friend when I picked up the receiver,
"you lost your taw?"

"How's that?"

"You misplace all your marbles? Your wife just told me you were out somewhere stalking a wasp with a rifle."

So I lied. I said it was just a little joke, that by chance I had recently slain a wasp while shooting at a target. He seemed satisfied, but I don't trust him. Newspaper people are the biggest gossips on earth. Even now the story may be spreading. A perfectly legitimate enterprise may be exaggerated and misinterpreted until it has an evil effect, reflecting on my character and mental condition, so much so that people might conclude that I actually *have* lost my taw.

I choose, therefore, to set down the true facts. About a year ago a neighbor of mine with a large wooded estate asked me if I enjoyed shooting small game and if I would care to join him for a morning of sport. I begged to be excused. I am one of those off-beat humans, possessing a lily liver and a chicken heart, who have no appetite for the slaughtering of deer, partridge, rabbits, squirrels or even woodchucks. I'm not militant about it, not intolerant toward those who do it—just personally squeamish.

"How about crows?" he suggested. "Like to shoot some crows?"

"No," I said. "I'll shoot pool. I'll shoot craps. I'll shoot golf. But no crows."

And I explained why. I won't shoot anything unless I have a fairly powerful grudge against it. Certainly I'll not shoot anything I admire, and I admire the crow. He has more sense than a lot of people I know. The fox is supposed to be smart but crows habitually outwit him in the forest. Crows can learn to talk English quicker than immigrants and they have a fine talent for mimicry. They can imitate chickens and dogs and owls and pigs and the New York Central whistling for the *Reader's Digest* crossing. If I had no other reason for admiring the crow, I would love him for the fact that, according to the Department of Agriculture, he eats poison ivy. Crows have a sense of humor, and they are deeply devoted to one another, and don't holler about it when they lay an egg, and take good care of their ailing and mourn their dead. They play ball games, have their own Mother's Day, hold elaborate court sessions when one of their boys transgresses the crow law, and post sentinels to warn against the approach of their enemies. If crows had hands I feel certain they would own television sets, and milk cows, and maintain checking accounts, and whistle with their fingers, and play the guitar.

"No," I said to my huntsman friend, "I'll race you to Walden Pond and back but I can't join you in any expedition aimed at destroying crows."

In my own theory a man ought to have an active dislike for the creature he goes out to shoot; I cannot quite fathom the philosophy of the citizen who stands with a bleeding pheasant in his hand and says, "Look at him! Ain't he a beauty!"

℮

There is, however, a living creature that I dislike, whose presence on my property is intolerable. I have reference to the wasp. I have been conducting a frenetic war against him for five years, simply because I am afraid of him. I've got so I can face an escaped convict or a motorcycle cop or a television camera without trembling, but let a wasp come within two or three feet of me and chills, as the song has it, run up and down my spine. Such being the case, I have no love for wasps and would force the varmints into slavery if I knew how.

It took a long time for me to find an effective method of dealing with this enemy. There were moments when I judged him to be immortal. Once I captured a sickly wasp that I found stumbling around the dining room. I prepared a solution of DDT, rotenone, kerosene, cayenne pepper and bourbon whisky. I took the wasp and folded him into this meringue, then I stirred vigorously. In a few minutes he surfaced, shook himself in the manner of a wet terrier, and made for me. I bellowed like the Mount Kisco fire signal and took cover, and saw him assault a chromo portrait of my wife at the age of five.

Another time I tried the string-and-flypaper technique which I found described in a book about country living. I managed to get a string over the roof of the house. On one end of it I fastened a sheet of flypaper. Then I went around to the other side of the house and pulled on the string until the flypaper was suspended just below the eaves where the wasps were living. Now I put on thick gauntlets and a homemade beekeeper's hat, mounted a stepladder until I was a foot or so from the nest, and began beating on a dishpan with a spoon. The book said the wasps would all fly out, even the children, head straight for the flypaper and entrap themselves. They flew out but they ignored the flypaper and made directly for me, giving off sizzling noises, with the consequence that I fell off the ladder. I glanced up just in time to see them heading into the woods looking for a caribou to whip.

Last summer conditions grew almost unbearable with the arrival in large numbers of a new kind of wasp. Wasps, like people, are divided into two main categories—the social and the solitary. The thing that they have in common is a stinger loaded with venom and an apparent lust to use it against me. Last summer's newcomers were solitary wasps —enormous bugs, big enough to bring down a barn owl or even a barn. I judged these horrifying beasts to be digger wasps, so denominated from the fact that they dig holes in the ground and stuff those holes full of dead enemies—grasshoppers, locusts, crows, sheep, Boy Scouts, and so on. I have not been stung by one of these digger wasps as yet, though I'm told that when one of them gets his hypo into a human, that human becomes as numb as a boulder.

There are people who love digger wasps and wouldn't hit one for money. There may even be a Wasp Society whose membership will pass resolutions against me for my heartless attitude toward their little (big) friends. Out in Milwaukee there were some people named Peckham who devoted hours and days and weeks to watching digger wasps, studying their habits, jotting down notes about their home life. In all the literature I have read on this subject, one major discrepancy appears. The wasp writers simply ignore the single detail that is important to me—the fact that a wasp has a stinger. They will describe every aspect of a wasp's physical construction and neglect to mention that stinger. It is much the same as the campaign biography which fails to mention that the noble character depicted in its pages will steal any money he can get his hands on. One widely popular insect book doesn't come any closer to the salient fact than to say that wasps are "irritable." Irritable, hell! They'll put you in the hospital with one bite!

Having employed every method I could think of in an effort to cope with the digger invasion, I finally hit upon the idea of shooting. I bought a gun and laid in a supply of ammunition. And I soon found that I had stumbled upon a sport that is fully as satisfying as shooting croquet, playing badminton, or gunning for wapiti.

A word as to the equipment needed. Personally I use a lever-action Daisy Carbine, Red Ryder Model No. 40, made in Plymouth, Michigan. For ammunition, I prefer copper-coated steel BB shot. This is not the BB shot of my boyhood—the soft lead type that would flatten slightly on contact with the forehead of another boy. The steel shot is preferable in wasp shooting for the reason that a wasp hasn't enough body to warrant use of a dum-dum BB. Moreover, a wasp knows how to slip blows as well as to roll with a punch, so you have got to hit him squarely and shatter him.

Shooting digger wasps requires the patience of a cat. The hunter must post himself within range of the wasp's burrow and get him as he comes out or as he arrives with the groceries. My first two weeks of sport were devoted to the diggers and at the end of that period there were none left. The ones I didn't bring down finally concluded that my land was indeed a hard and bitter country to settle, and they had gone on to Mr. Buttolph's or Mr. Avery's.

☺

Now a strange thing happened. The mysterious fever that seizes the huntsman took hold of me. I was unhappy because I had no more digger wasps to shoot. I couldn't go to my neighbors and ask permission to shoot wasps on their land. They already think I'm a trifle queer from the fact that I sometimes employ a water pistol loaded with DDT to shoot Japanese beetles. I was reduced to gunning for ordinary, or social, wasps. I began by shooting them at the swimming pool. During the hot part of the summer they flew around the pool, alighting at the water's edge to drink. These wasps are perhaps one-fifth the size of the diggers and that much harder to hit. Consequently my marksmanship improved day by day. I learned, for one thing, that it is foolish to aim directly at the animal itself. The shot should be placed about a quarter of an inch in front of him, so that it gets him on the bounce or ricochet. I stalked wasps beside the pool for about a week and before long found that I could bring down my bug on the first shot, provided he held still. If I missed, he sometimes attempted a retaliatory assault, charging at me with his hinder fang bared. But there is an element of danger in every adventuresome sport, else the fun would go out of it, so I accepted counter-attack as part of the game, and always kept a Ping-pong paddle at my side to bat off assailants.

Before long the wasps quit the water hole and gave ground, retiring to the house. I began shooting them off the house until my wife stopped me, pointing out the chips and dents and reminding me how I howled when I got the bill for the paint job. I looked around for new fields in which to practice my sport, and found a veritable wasp heaven.

It happens that I am famous locally as a grower of cucumbers and one end of my garden is given over to the vines. I discovered that wasps have an affinity for cucumbers. I don't know the reason, though I assume that they move from leaf to leaf, eating off aphids and boll weevils and cankerworms and cucumber thrips. It would seem, at first glance, a gross injustice for me to shoot wasps in my cucumber patch when those wasps were out there doing me a service. I didn't look at it that way. In the first place, I got the other fellow's point of view—put myself in the place of the wasps. They were doing me no favors—they were out there engaged in a wholly selfish act, stuffing their own greedy gizzards. And in the second place, I'm sick of cucumbers. I *want* the aphids and the boll weevils and the thrips to sweep through that patch, gnaw those vines to the ground, wipe out the crop, create a cucumber famine on my property.

It was mid-August when I started firing into the cucumber patch, spending an hour or two each day beside the garden fence, smashing the brown varmints to smithereens the moment they showed their antenna, shooting steadily until callers arrived, or delivery men, at which periods I'd quickly conceal the gun beneath the breezeway steps and pretend that I'd been out sharpening a sickle. I realized full well what my friends and neighbors would think—it's the sort of thing that can destroy a man's reputation. "Smith? Sure, I know him. Sets up there all day long with a BB gun, shootin' at wasps in his cucumber patch. We got all kinds up this way."

For a while I bought my ammunition in small paper tubes, at ten cents a tube, but this practice proved a nuisance so I went to the hardware store and asked if they didn't have BB shot in bulk—I wanted to buy it by the peck. They scratched around back of some old blowtorches and came up with some one-pound packages and now, as I face the new wasp season, I have an adequate ammunition dump. And I find myself in a paradoxical frame of mind. I started shooting wasps to get rid of them, and now I am hoping that bigger and wilder wasps select my premises for their feeding ground in 1961.

There is one after-effect that I must mention. The cucumbers remaining in my patch when I first started shooting there were all riddled with BB shot and ruined. When the season was over I simply threw them all away. The beets were what caused the trouble. Off to one side of the cucumber patch I had a half dozen rows of beets. The cucumber vines had encroached on the territory belonging to the beets and in firing at wasps in that particular area, the angle had been just right for the BB to wipe out a wasp and then plunge into a beet. In time the beets were harvested and cooked and pickled and put into jars. Inevitably it had to be a guest in our home who bit the first BB. It was a student of hotel management from Cornell. He cracked a filling, then fished the offending article out of his mouth, held it between thumb and forefinger and scrutinized it closely.

"What on earth!" he murmured. I saw the glint of copper coating and knew what it was, but didn't say anything. "It looks like . . ." he went on, ". . . do you suppose it's possible that a beet could absorb, out of the ground, a little gold nugget . . . ?"

I told him what it was and put his mind at rest. Through the remainder of the winter we ate the beets, chewing them in a gingerly and tentative manner and spitting out the BB's. We could have thrown the whole batch of beets away but, after all, one must be prepared to make certain little sacrifices, to put up with minor discomforts, if one is determined to be a true sportsman.

Note: I want it understood that while I am insecticidal, I am well-disposed toward almost all other animal life. I am on record elsewhere as being violently opposed to the slaughter of bulls in the *corrida de toros.* A few days ago I was reading a newspaper report on a bullfight in Spain and I came upon a delightful typographical error. This is what it said: "The bull turned and snotted at the spectators." I think I'd have done it, too, if I'd have been there.

[141]

FALL

———❖———

> Hurricanes are a major problem on the At-
> lantic Coast. In solving that problem, let us
> first consider the fact that most of them occur
> in August and September. The solution? Do
> away with August and September.
>
> *—Sayings of Avery*

Climatology

[The Adam Bomb and Our Weather]

Sept. 12—Last week, on the coldest September 8th in history, a lady resident of Spring Valley wrote a letter to the
New York *Herald Tribune* saying:

> Many people I talk with seem to be sure that
> the strange and often terrible kinds of weather in
> most parts of the country are the results of atomic
> tests . . . If there is any truth in the theory, we
> should be informed about it—all of us.

I think I know what is in this lady's mind. All around
her she hears her neighbors blaming the atomic bomb for
wet spells, dry spells, hot spells, cold spells and even intoler-
ably dull spells of "seasonal" weather. She wants to be sure
of her ground before she joins the chorus. She is the only
person I know who is being cautious in the matter. Almost

[143]

everyone in my neighborhood *knows* that the bomb has fouled up the climate.

One of the great joys of life in democratic America stems from the privilege of blaming, in a loud voice, someone or something for any evil that visits us. We have the right to howl against high taxes and corruption and nepotism and eggheadery and the fact that the strawberries on the bottom of the box are never as nice as the strawberries on the top of the box. We also have the right to howl against the weather even though it is sometimes difficult to locate responsibility.

One evening during the wet spring this year, I went to the Yankee Stadium to watch the New York Yankees try to play a game of baseball. They made it into the second inning and then the rain began to fall, gently at first.

I was sitting in the stands back of third base and directly in front of me was a large gentleman in a pork-pie hat. As the raindrops started falling this gentleman wrenched his head back and glared into the black sky. Then he said, "Boo!" A moment later it began raining harder, and several other gentlemen in our section yelled "Boo!" The party in the pork-pie hat now realized that his original complaint had not intimidated the clouds, but he was in a damp fury and he howled, "Boooooo! Ya bum ya!"

His mood of angry defiance spread swiftly through the stands, the crowd got to its feet and one of those long choral boos, so common to the national pastime, rose above the stadium. It was the only time I have ever witnessed mob action against the weather. There was something weird about it, and weird things disturb me, so I tried to find some logic in the crowd's behavior. It didn't seem reasonable to believe that those people were booing moisture. I can get mad at mud, but not to the extent of hitting it with a blackjack. Yet the feeling in that crowd, engendered by so many ball games being rained out, was of the same temper as that which precedes the formation of a posse of honest ranchers. I half expected those thousands of fans to suddenly leap on horses and go riding off in pursuit of gutter-water.

As it turned out, they grumbled their way out of the park, for the game had to be postponed, and I got my car and started home, still puzzling over the mysterious attitudes which human beings hold toward the weather.

For a while I thought I had the answer. Those people had been booing the employees of the United States Weather Bureau, known collectively as the Weather Man. In the human brain there is a bare space lying between the conscious and the subconscious which causes people to blame the Weather Man for unfavorable weather. He is cursed and abused for blizzards as well as for heat waves. So, my speculation about mud could have been wrong. It is altogether possible that people have gotten so mad at mud that they've taken a club to it. We sometimes kick the automobile because the battery has gone dead, we cuss the hammer that hits our thumb, and we shatter a radio set because a man in a studio says something we don't like.

It came to me that I'm as guilty as the others. That little gap in the brain is tricky and, on occasion, I have found myself assuming a most unreasonable attitude toward the Weather Man. One day I was watching him on my television screen, working up a weather map, drawing those chalk lines and scratching down cryptic legends, such as "scat. sh." and "ptly. cl." and "f. o. b. Detroit." I listened to his learned talk about occluded fronts in purple, and surface temperature discontinuities, and dewpoint. I may have been a bit drowsy at the moment, or even demented, for the impression came to me that the Weather Man was drawing those heavy, curving lines to *box in* highs and lows and fronts and backs. I had a vague feeling that those chalk lines were fences to hold back the climate, and that the wind howled up and down between them and couldn't get out. Please don't tell me I was right, because I came to the conclusion that I was a victim of Frithiof's Law. I can illustrate the workings of Frithiof's Law with two examples:

1. A city woman visits a farm in the country and is taken out to see the pigs being slopped. She watches the animals in their greedy snuffling and snorting at the trough, and then observes: "My gracious! No *wonder* they call them pigs!"

2. A young man engaged in scientific studies at Fordham University stumbles against the university's seismograph. The jolt causes the needle to jiggle sharply and brings on a terrible earthquake 2,800 miles south of New York City, in Venezuela.

Under Frithiof's Law, anybody who would hit mud is being unreasonable, and if those people in the Polo Grounds were hooting the Weather Man, they were acting unintelligently. I find it impossible to believe that baseball fans are lacking in intelligence, so I began searching elsewhere for an answer, and found it. Their derision was not aimed at the Weather Man. They were booing the Atomic Energy Commission.

℃

The atomic bomb has superseded all other agencies as a blamable source of bad weather. The recent history of popular climatology in our section begins with the 1950 water famine in New York City, at which time a scientist was given an airplane and some dry ice and sent out to seed clouds. His efforts to fill the city's reservoirs were not too successful but, in the opinion of a great many citizens, he fouled up the atmosphere over the whole Middle Atlantic seaboard. He brought on summers that were too hot, or too cold; autumns that were too cold, or too hot; winters that were abnormally severe, or so warm that everybody caught the flu. He was blamed because vegetables grew too slow and weeds grew too fast and mosquitoes stung harder and smallpox vaccinations wouldn't take and the mailman was late three days in a row. Then he was rescued from all this abuse by the woolly bear.

The woolly bear is a worm in a fur coat. Somebody decided that the disposition of the brown and black fur segments on the worm's body were a true indication of winter weather to come. People forgot the cloud-seeder, threw away their almanacs, and went hog-wild about woolly bears. That is, until the winter of 1952–1953. That autumn the fur on the worm foretold a long and brutal winter and everyone rushed out and bought extra weather-stripping and snow shovels and earmuffs, and then the winter turned out to be extraordinarily temperate. It was, in fact, one of the mildest winters we've had in years. The woolly bears themselves spent the whole winter lolling around in the warm grass, which was another demonstration of bad judgment on their part because a few disgruntled citizens kicked at them and called them names. They were not accused of inability to foretell weather; they were charged with malicious fraud and deliberate deceit. Yet there had to be an explanation for the mild winter, and the sopping spring that followed, so now the nuclear fission theory of weather derangement began to pick up steam.

☺

Personally, I have been inclined to stick with the straight scientific attitude and blame the Weather Man because he seems more vulnerable than either worms or the atomic bomb. I was watching him one morning when he was trying to draw a picture of a high pressure area—a difficult thing to do because it is so far up, and even then it is nothing but air. True, it is agitated air, but agitated air, at a distance, looks exactly the same to me as limp air. The Weather Man did his best with this problem and then shrugged and backtracked westward across two chalk lines and somewhere in the Mississippi Valley he jotted down "anti cy." I grabbed up my weather manual, which I keep beside the television set, and checked the index and found that he had reference to an "anticyclone." Normally I would assume that an anticyclone would be another name for a citizen of Arkansas, but it isn't. It's an extensive horizontal movement of the atmosphere spirally around and away from a gradually progressing central region of high barometric pressure, the spiral motion being clockwise in the Northern Hemisphere, counterclockwise in the Southern, put down eight and carry three.

I already knew this, of course, but what I didn't know was that an anticyclone can be judged under Buys Ballot's Law provided you live in the Northern Hemisphere. I checked that, too, and found I was eligible. The book said it was a simple matter. You go outdoors and stand facing the wind. The atmospheric pressure decreases toward your right and increases toward your left and thus indicates the direction of the center of the anticyclone.

I tried it. I went out and faced the wind and then inspected the atmospheric pressure on my right. It was pretty weak, all right, while the pressure on my left was, by my own quick estimate, sufficient to lift twelve horses forty-

[148]

six feet in the air, upside down over Delaware. So far, so good. The next step was to find out what direction the center of the anticyclone was taking. The manual failed to explain, to my own satisfaction, how this was accomplished, and I was pretty sore about it, having gone to all that bother, so I telephoned the weather station over at Bear Mountain. They said the man was out looking at woolly bears and wouldn't be back till dinnertime, so I called the Weather Bureau in Manhattan and they said, rather condescendingly, I thought, that there weren't any anticyclones in our area at the moment and what I thought was high pressure was probably nothing more than a slight infection in the Eustachian tube of my left ear. So I pounded my head with the heel of my hand and went back to the television set just in time to hear the man say it would be fair today and fair tomorrow. A few minutes later Hysee, the cleaning woman, came in the back door.

"I don't think," she said, "that I'll wash the windows on the outside today. It's gonna rain tomorrow." I asked her how she knew. "The dog's out there in the yard eating grass," she said. "Any time you see a dog eating grass, it's a sign it's gonna rain tomorrow."

The next day it rained for nine hours and my unswerving devotion to the Weather Man began to swerve a little. Since then I have been getting most of my weather lore from Hysee (short for Hyacinth) and from Bruno, a short, fat man who looks a good deal like the late W. C. Fields and who comes to my place occasionally to perform certain outside chores. The two of them, Hysee and Bruno, furnish me with an accurate reflection of the current popular beliefs concerning Nature's consistent inconsistency.

Bruno believes that the mildness of last winter was a direct consequence of the "tonic" bomb.

"All you got to do," he says, "is watch it. Everytime they shoot off one of them tonic bombs, the weather goes out of its head. It ruined the whole winter."

"How do you mean, ruined?" I asked.

"Winters," he said, "was made to be cold."

Hysee refers to the same explosive agency when she speaks of the "Adam" bomb, to which she attributes various unnatural disturbances, mostly indoors. Several years ago we had an infestation of ladybugs in our area. Trillions of them. They didn't bite anybody or damage anything and, as a matter of fact, I rather enjoyed their coming, for they gave a pleasant speckled effect to the wallpaper and the window panes. Hysee, however, treated them as enemies.

"They were blowed over here," she said, "by the Adam bomb."

"From where?" I wanted to know.

"Out there," she said, waving a hand in a southwesterly direction.

"Well," I said, "let's leave them alone. People say they won't hurt anything."

"You don't know ladybugs," said Hysee. "They won't hurt nothing for a while because they're too dizzy to eat. Give them a few weeks to get their breath back and they'll crunch this whole house down."

I let her have her way with the ladybugs. She worked on them with ammonia, and bug bombs, and vacuumed them up by the peck, and still they came, so finally she gave up. She said the only way we'd ever get rid of them would be to shoot off another Adam bomb, this time up close. That would blow them out in the ocean and they'd all drown. I didn't bother to mention that we would go with them. Anyway, they finally left of their own accord and we have all but forgotten them. Meanwhile Hysee has continued to feed me information on the disturbing effects of the Adam bomb in other directions. She knows a well-to-do lady who lives on the other side of town and who has to shave her upper lip every two days because, since they started shooting off the Adam bomb, she has grown a mustache. Hysee also says that the birds are beginning to get hoarse, for the reason that they've got radium in them. "It's from eating fish," she says. "The fish got radium in them from the Adam bomb, and the birds eat the fish, and they get radium in them, and if you got a good ear for birds, you'll notice that they are beginning to get hoarse."

Bruno has gone over to the tonic bomb school of thought with some reluctance, for he continues as a strong adherent of the woolly bears. He has not given up on them. He admits that they failed miserably last winter, but he explains that it was a simple case of a worm not being able to buck a tonic bomb. If they'd just quit shooting off the tonic bombs, then the woolly bears would soon get our winters under control. Bruno contends that the wet spring was an effort on the part of the woolly bears to make up for their winter failure.

Hysee says Bruno is a nit-wit. "Them little worms," she says, "don't know a thing about winter. You want to know about the kind of winter it's going to be, give me a goosebone. Give me the breastbone of a wild goose that's been killed in October, and I'll tell you what kind of winter to expect, all depending on the size and the shape and the color and all."

The goosebone tells her only how *cold* the winter will be. She has another tried-and-true method for determining what to expect in the way of snow and rain. She takes a large onion and cuts it in half and, removing the layers, acquires twelve little onion cups. She lines these up on a table and gives them the names of the months, beginning with the current month. She puts a large pinch of salt in the bottom of each onion cup and lets them stand overnight. In the morning, the one containing the greatest accumulation of water tells her which month will have the most rain or snow. "Prissipation, it's called," she explained to me. "If it's winter, the prissipation will be snow. Elsewhere it will be rain."

I'm sold. It's a much more colorful way of judging weather than the system of trying to feel pressure with your Eustachian tubes. Hysee has told me that down in the village she heard that "funny lumps" are beginning to appear on the sidewalls of automobile tires right after each explosion of the Adam bomb. I don't offer this to the lady in Spring Valley as incontrovertible evidence. I do recommend to her that she inspect her tires for funny lumps, that she listen for hoarseness in the birds, and watch for a growth of hair on her upper lip. These things may help her toward a better understanding of the Adam bomb and its relationship toward weather. I have heard that the Atomic Energy Commission has denied that it is responsible for eccentricities of the weather. I choose to go along with the sovereign people and their interpretation of Nature's capricious ways. I have always enjoyed the story of the two astronomers. One of them is crouched over, peering into the world's biggest telescope—an instrument the size of the Chrysler tower.

"It's going to rain," he says to his colleague.

"How can you tell?"

"My corns hurt."

The Asking Price

Sept. 17–Let's have a brief look at the commonplace phrase, "asking price," as it is employed in the real estate business. It is not the price that the owner expects to get for his property. I have been told that at no time in the history of the world has anybody ever paid the asking price for a piece of property. That, of course, is not true but it is a rare bird who does pay it. A man who has a house to sell figures out what he wants to get for it—say twenty thousand dollars.

So he puts an "asking price" of twenty-five thousand on it. Along comes a prospective buyer and looks the property over and finally he says to the owner, "Well, how much?" The owner then says, "I'm asking twenty-five thousand." And the prospect says, "Yeh. I know. But how much you want for it?" Whereupon the owner says, "Twenty thousand."

What the hell kind of a fumadiddlin' way of doing business is that? I suppose the whole theory of the "asking price" is based on the idea that every now and then a colossal sucker comes along, one who doesn't understand the science of "asking prices" and who will pay the first figure quoted him without haggling. If he does, then the way I see it he is being swindled out of—to use the cited example—a clean five thousand dollars. He is paying five thousand bucks more than the property is worth—at least.

Martha Sleeper's Housewarming

Sept. 20—Martha Sleeper, the former actress, is now one of the most prominent women in Puerto Rico, where she operates a fashionable shop for women. She formerly lived in these parts and I remember her best for the housewarming she gave.

She had made all arrangements about food and drinks and music and the guest list kept growing and then she began to worry about parking space for all the cars. An inspiration came. The house across the road was vacant and had plenty of parking space, so she phoned the real estate agent who had it listed and asked if her guests could leave their cars there. He said it was all right. So Martha fixed a sign and went across the road to post it, and then inspected the parking area, and after that found a door open in the big vacant house and went in to have a look at it. There was no furniture in it but it had large rooms and pretty light fixtures and nice woodwork. Martha thought: "I've got *my* house all organized, all fixed with new things. Why should I have these people come piling in and wrecking it? They'll all get drunk and spill things and break furniture." So she moved the music and the bar and the buffet over to the vacant house and held her housewarming there.

> I resent being called an abnormal drinker
> because to me, abnormal drinking is normal.
> —*Sayings of Avery*

Charcoal Broil

[Cookouts Can Be Murder]

Sept. 29—The other day I got out my portable barbecue grill and set it up on the back terrace. I filled the pan with a triple layer of charcoal briquets, squirted some charcoal lighter fluid over the briquets and set them afire.

A little while later, the Coogans arrived and I went into the kitchen and got the big steak. I was about to put it on the grill when Coogan, who had been quietly watching me from a distance of twenty feet (the sneak!) let out a yell. "Hold it!" he bellowed. "Good lord, man, you're not gonna put that meat on yet, are you? That fire's not ready, not by a long shot."

I thought the coals were about right but I'm a timid soul in the presence of authority so I withheld operations for another fifteen minutes. During that time Coogan cross-examined me about my charcoal and told me I was an idiot to buy briquets. He asked if I had marinated the meat, and when I said I had, he told me that was probably a mistake. He asked me to name the ingredients of the marinade. I did so, and he grimaced and said the steak would taste like a slab of mutton with two coats of varnish.

At last, when I picked up the meat and prepared to plop it onto the grill, Coogan screeched anew—this time so suddenly that I dropped the steak on the ground. "Jesus God!" he cried, "don't you know you gotta rub that grill with suet? Your meat will stick to it like glue!" At that instant I quietly but firmly resolved that Coogan would never again be invited to partake of groceries at my house—indoors or out.

The enormous increase in alfresco cookery in the last ten years is one of the more pleasant social phenomena of our times, but it has brought with it a virulent form of kibitzing that in some cases has resulted in feuds and vendettas that make the Hatfield-McCoy squabble look like a schoolgirl hair-pull.

The cookout, as everyone knows, belongs to the men and represents an atavistic return to Neanderthal man and his campfire and to our own frontiersman with his fire of buffalo chips. Men who wouldn't dream of heating a can of soup on the kitchen stove leap to the outdoor grill with boyish eagerness and complain bitterly if their wives so much as prod the meat they are cooking.

And the wives—how they are laughing behind their hands! For years beyond number, men have been snickering over the way women gossip and gibble-gabble about each other, but now, with the cookout, retribution has set in. The home barbecue has turned many of our men into grouches and common scolds. I have a friend who is president of a corporation in New York City. Not long ago he had a cookout at noontime on a Saturday. One of his guests, an advertising man, sharply criticized his use of lighter fluid on the charcoal, saying it would ruin the taste of the meat. On the following Monday, the corporation president's wife told my wife: "Fred sulked all Saturday evening and all day Sunday because of what Jack said about the lighter fluid. He says he's going to take his account away from Jack's company."

Thus far I've been able to keep in the clear, probably because I've given some thought to the dangers inherent in cookout criticism. Not long after the Coogan affair I was invited to the Shaughnessy's for Sunday lunch. When I arrived, Shaughnessy was already broiling the chicken on his outdoor grill. The simpleton wasn't using enough charcoal, and for the amount he had, his grill wasn't set at the correct distance from the coals (I don't think the clod *knew* he could adjust the grill to whatever level he wanted). I was on the verge of giving him some advice, in the form of soft suggestions rather than the raucous criticisms of a Coogan, but I thought of Coogan and kept quiet. Then Mrs. Shaughnessy yelled from the kitchen door that she was ready, and Shaughnessy began taking up the chicken. Apparently the poor jerk didn't have the nerve to tell his wife the chicken wasn't done—or, more likely, he wasn't capable of judging *when* a chicken is done—so in a few minutes we were trying to eat chicken that hadn't even been scorched, pink meat of a sickening, rubbery consistency. I wanted desperately to give Shaughnessy a sound lecture on the art of the cookout— just for his own good, mind you—but again I held my tongue.

℃

Please don't get the idea that I am one of those finicky, overfastidious sort of outdoor chefs. I'm pretty haphazard and slapdash at my cooking, but I'm well acquainted with the basic rules of the game. I've been cooking outdoors for twenty years, yet in common with most Americans I didn't take it up in a big way until after World War II. When I bought my house fifteen years ago, I spent a small fortune having a barbecue built of flagstone with a handsome walled terrace surrounding it. This barbecue has two grills and an elegant tapering chimney and I have not had a fire in it for the last five or six years. Outdoor cookery really achieved its great upsurge with the coming of the portable grill. Most of us in my rural neighborhood switched to portable grills after a paralyzing ice storm that hit us some years ago. Glare ice, almost two inches thick, covered the roads and drive-ways and fields—walking was almost impossible, driving was out of the question, and for four days we had no electricity. I kept a roaring fire going in the house night and day and built a makeshift stove in the fireplace, using bricks and the big iron grill from the fieldstone barbecue. By candlelight, I assembled a potful of chili con carne and cooked it in the fireplace and it was the best chili con carne I've made in thirty years of chili-making. The real triumph, however, was our extraordinary strawberry shortcake. My wife found a package of strawberries in the freezer compartment. They were thawing fast and so we boldly decided on a shortcake. She explained to me that in order to bake the cake part, a medium heat is needed. So I had her mix the dough and put it in a pie pan. I set a brick on end, on top of the fireplace grill, and balanced the pie pan on top of the brick. It baked perfectly, and there in the chill and semi-darkness, sans lights and sans radio and sans TV and sans electric blankets, iso-lated from the world, we enjoyed steaming hot chili, with delicious strawberry shortcake for dessert. The only achieve-ment equal to ours was that of a neighbor, a young lawyer, who had no fireplace in his house but located two cans of Sterno. He set three empty beer cans on the floor in a triangular pattern, put the burning Sterno in the middle and set his skillet on top of the beer cans.

The ice storm taught us that big stationary outdoor grills were something of a nuisance, and we all bought the portable kind, and began cooking outdoors almost as much as we cooked indoors. The big stone or brick grills were forgotten. One friend of mine, a successful novelist without a shred of common sense, bought an enormous house and decided that his outdoor barbecue should be of commensurate dimensions, so he had two of them built, side by side and almost as big as cathedrals, capable of burning tree-length logs. When Truth came to him at last and the small, portable grill became standard, he had concrete roofs put over his two huge barbecues and converted them into doghouses. His chagrin and disappointment grew even greater when his dogs refused to enter them.

☺

The extent of outdoor cookery today becomes apparent to anyone who happens to drive an automobile through any suburban area in the United States on a Saturday evening, say around seven o'clock. In almost every block, if the wind is right, there comes wafting on the breeze the lovely redolence of steak being burned to a crisp. And, perhaps, male voices raised in heated dispute —for that has become part of the game.

Even such an even-tempered man as James Beard, the celebrated gourmet, grows livid when he contemplates certain methods of outdoor cookery as practiced in the Republic today. "Some of the deeds performed in the name of grilling or broiling outdoors," he says, "are grounds for divorce and a just and legitimate reason for homicide." He mentions in particular one man who covers his steak with brown sugar before putting it on the fire, another who smears his meat with Roquefort cheese and butter, and still another who applies a coating of flour, water and herbs.

Mr. Beard's judgment reminds me of the Gillfords, who have been married for seventeen years and who are known to all their friends as the most happily wed couple in the county. Once I asked Effie if it were true, as reported, that they had never had a quarrel. "We've not only had quarrels," she said, "but we've had several pretty serious fights." I asked what they were about. "Well," she said, "we've never exchanged a harsh word over but one thing —Bob's way of messing up dinner when he's cooking outdoors. He either starts the fire too early, and the meat is ready before the table is set or the salad made, or he starts the fire too late so that half the guests get pie-eyed and don't want to eat. We have quarreled over that one single thing, and once I got so mad that I threw a pan of melted garlic butter at him."

In my years of cooking out and attending other cook-outs I have noted the various sore points which bring on the disputes and sometimes result in two men quitting speaking to each other.

The quality of the charcoal is a common cause of arguments. There are men who buy their charcoal with much more meticulosity than they employ in buying their meat. They labor under a terrible incubus—the fear that they'll get hold of some charcoal made from pine, or that there will be a little bit of pine charcoal mixed in with the hardwood. They contend that if there's any pine in the charcoal, the fire will sputter and burn unevenly and throw sparks and, worst of all, the meat will taste of pine. (I know one man who answers this argument with, "Damn it all, I *like* the taste of pine!") These are the men who are opposed to briquets, claiming that they are made from a variety of woods with a good portion of the hated pine mixed in. Adherents of briquets, it must be pointed out, say this is a dirty lie.

There are devotees who contend that the charcoal is as important in outdoor cookery as the herbs and spices in indoor cookery. They say that they "develop a taste" for charcoal made from a specific kind of wood and that no other kind of wood will do. Some "develop a taste" for hickory, some for oak, some for apple, maple, cherry, and in Florida there's a man who won't eat barbecued meat unless it has been cooked with wood from the lemon tree. There are other men who, being uncertain about the quality of their charcoal, buy chips of, say, applewood, soak them in water so they'll give off a heavy smoke, then sprinkle them over their fire with the consequence, I imagine, that their chicken comes out tasting pretty much like a big red apple.

In the days before canned charcoal lighter fluid, I was always quite casual about the way I laid my fire and got it started. Today there's a school of thought which places great emphasis on the way a fire is laid. One man I know spends almost as much time laying the fire as he takes to cook a steak. He puts in carefully crumpled paper, then little sticklets of kindling wood that look as if they'd been measured with calipers, and then the charcoal, which is not dumped into the pan, but placed in one piece at a time, carefully, to make certain there are adequate air spaces between the pieces.

Methods for cooking sweet corn provoke a good many arguments. One man will say that the outer layers of the husks should be stripped off, and the ears then placed on the back of the grill. Another will insist that the husks be left on, dampened with salted water and placed on the bed of coals where they should be turned frequently. Still another belongs to the aluminum foil school, saying the husks should be removed, the ears smeared with butter and wrapped in foil and placed on the coals.

Some people employ a water sprinkler, or a rubber squirting device known as a *spritzer,* for the purpose of slowing down the fire and at the same time creating more smoke; others say that putting water on a charcoal fire is a criminal offense common only to pedigreed morons.

There is also the question of the chef's hat and the apron with the comical inscriptions, such as "Come 'n' Get It!" and "Just Call Me Escoffier!" and the big pocket labeled "Tips." Some men insist on wearing these costumes, believing that they are contributing to the good feeling of the party; others describe the wearers of cap-and-apron as chuckleheads who ought to be committed.

❧

Not long ago at a cookout in New Jersey, I saw two men almost come to blows over the matter of turning a steak on the grill. The host emerged from the house with a pair of tongs, designed especially for this very job. The other man, his guest, flew into a loud fret. "Never," he said, "never, never, never touch your meat with any metal instrument. Never, *never,* NEVER!"

"Poppycock!" exclaimed the host. "How do you expect me to turn it over—with my feet?"

"The proper procedure, recommended by famous chefs," explained the guest, "is to put on a pair of clean white gloves and take hold of the steak and flip it over with your fingers. *Don't ever use a fork or tongs or any other metal instrument!"*

To which the host replied, with considerable asperity, *"Don't ever come over here and tell me how to cook a steak!"* And using the tongs, he turned the steak. I doubt if those two men see much of each other any more.

It is possible today to spend a fortune on equipment for outdoor cooking; the grills themselves come in many shapes and sizes, and there are elaborate barbecue wagons with shelves and warming ovens and chopping boards and spits turned by electricity that run into hundreds of dollars. These expensive setups come with various accessories, including even skewers and swords. Most men, I find, are not impressed by the shish-kebabber who cooks and serves his meat on rods or swords. I'm reminded of the time Jimmy Durante took Martha Raye for her first visit to the Pump Room in Chicago—a great place for sword-cookery. They were sitting talking when a waiter came down the line bearing aloft a chunk of flaming meat on the tip of a sword. Miss Raye let out a startled yelp and exclaimed, "What in the world is that?" To which Mr. Durante replied, "That's a man who made the mistake of tippin' only a dollar."

As I said before, I've been cooking out for many years and the principal frustration I suffer is that of a beautiful fire going to waste. I always have a feeling that my fire is swiftly dying when all the black parts are gone from the charcoal. I feel that I'm faced with disaster, that the coals are growing cool before I even get my meat on the grill. Consequently I usually defy the rules and start cooking before all the black spots disappear. And I'm usually finished at about the time the coals reach perfection. Thereafter, for a couple of hours, I look at those glowing coals and curse myself for having hurried, and I always say, "If we only had something else to cook—just look at that beautiful fire going to waste!" I happen to know that many of my friends and neighbors are guilty of the same mismanagement and that they, too, groan about the wasted fire. I have thought about laying in a supply of green coffee beans and roasting some of them after I've removed the meat; I've even thought of roasting peanuts.

In the interests of benign social intercourse there has long been a rule that says: Never poke another man's fire if you would retain his friendship. Even more important today, I think, is the need for a rule that says: Never kibitz another man's outdoor cookery unless you desire a slug in the puss. I try to follow that rule and I recommend the procedure I have worked out for myself. If the temptation to criticize grows too strong I walk away from the grill, go into the house and put a record on the hi-fi. If they have it, I favor Fats Waller singing, *You Run Your Mouth and I'll Run My Business, Brother!*

Interior Decoration

Sept. 30–Avery, my neighbor, used to insist on doing occasional paint jobs himself, but he has decided to paint nothing but floors and leave the rest to the professionals. He was redecorating his downstairs bathroom when I stopped in today, and he asked me a question which surely deserves to be among the immortal queries of all time:

"How on earth do you keep the paint out of your armpits?"

He had been doing the bathroom ceiling in rumpled

maroon, and his wife told me he could not get it through his head that in this type of work, one never dips the brush into the paint more than about half an inch. He'd dip it clear to the handle, then raise his right arm above his head, and the paint would run down the brush handle and down his arm and into his armpit.

"This," he told me, "is one of the worst nuisances I ever encountered. I'll be glad when this ceiling's done. I can't wait to get to the floor. I was cut out to be a floor painter."

———◆◆———

The Morro Castle Spoon

Sept. 30–Our bachelor-girl friend Marie came to me recently with what she considers to be a slightly psychiatric problem. I am personally somewhat daft myself, yet people do approach me with their troubles. Marie says she believes she is turning into a frightful snob. She goes into New York City once or twice a week for dinner with friends, and very often they dine at one of the plush joints. It is Marie's custom to fetch match books away from these high class restaurants and on her coffee table at home she has a basket piled high with these match books. Lately she says this thing has been happening to her. She'll pick up a match book from, say, Le Pavillon or the Four Seasons or the Colony or Voisin and start toward the kitchen to light her oven. Suddenly she'll notice the name on the match book, and she'll decide that her lowly little oven should not be set going with matches from such an elegant establishment; and so she'll go back to the basket and pick out a match book from, perhaps, the Brass Rail or Schrafft's or Dominic Settiducatti's Bar & Grill, and use *that* for lighting her oven.

I told her she was not a victim of snobbism, but of habit.

I told her about my coffee spoon. Years ago when I was a young reporter, fresh out of the West, I went on a junket with other newspapermen aboard the Ward Line ship, *Morro Castle*, on its shakedown cruise. There was much drinking during the cruise, and the newspapermen held a contest to see which could steal the most off the ship before docking in New York. I didn't win, but I got away with a desk lamp and a spoon. The spoon is a pretty silver one, inscribed with the insignia of the Ward Line, and I still have it thirty years after the crime. As you doubtless know, the *Morro Castle* some years later burned off the Jersey shore in one of the nation's biggest maritime tragedies. But the desk lamp still burns in my office and I use that spoon every morning. Even when I'm still half asleep I'll grope around in the silver drawer to get the *Morro Castle* spoon—somehow it makes my coffee taste better. I have no intention of consulting a psychiatrist about this matter; I'm a little bit afraid to think about what it might mean. Only one thing is sure—it eased the mind of my friend Marie. She is satisfied that her oven should never be lighted with those fancy matches; she uses them only in the more aristocratic pursuit of starting the fire in her fireplace.

> I suspect all translations of place names with
> Indian origins. Abe Burrows speaks of a place
> called Spitting Rock, adding that "on this spot
> an Indian maid once spit all over her lover."
> —*Sayings of Avery*

Obituary

[Rufus]

Oct. 12—My most intimate friend died two days ago.

While the vet was putting him away, I went into the deep woods back of the house and wandered around for an hour, trying to fight off a sickish feeling and not succeeding at all. It was one of the worst hours I've ever had.

His name was Rufus and he had been my constant companion for all of the thirteen years of his life. He was a black cocker spaniel and during those years, from early morning to late at night, he was forever at my feet. As has been stated, my office is across a breezeway from the house and each morning, when I had finished breakfast, I'd address him as "Miss Blue"—recalling the secretary in the old Amos 'n' Andy radio show ("Miss Blue, buzz me!").

"All right, Miss Blue," I'd say, and head for the office, and he'd be right at my heels, ready for the day's work, ready to supervise everything I did. Sometimes there in the privacy of the office I'd talk to him. He was the first to

hear the plots of two novels I wrote. He never said anything, one way or another, even after the books came out. I
didn't expect him to. I didn't want him to. I wasn't looking
for critical comment—I simply wanted to talk about those
stories. He thought I was tetched. Whenever I talked to
him at some length, he would twist his head to one side and
keep it there, staring at me, telling me quite clearly that I
was off my rocker. It never bothered me, because a lot of
people look at me the same way.

On those occasions when I did leave the property for
an hour or a day or a week, he would plant himself in the
middle of the driveway and sit there staring patiently toward the road, until he heard my car horn beyond the
curve. He could distinguish my horn from a hundred others
and sometimes, on hearing it, he'd start racing around in a
circle—he was that happy over my return.

Rufus had faults and failings that were almost human.
He was, in fact, more of a "person" than many of my neighbors; he could be depended upon to react in certain definite
ways to certain definite stimuli. He was a real oddball in
many of his traits. For example, he was afraid of rabbits.
Several times in his later years I saw him skulk in the presence of a rabbit. There was a reason for it. When he was
younger he chased rabbits like any other dog. One day we
were going down the hill to the mailbox when a cottontail
took off across the field. Rufus gave it the old college try,
running as hard as he could, and then something happened to
his back legs. Both of them were somehow thrown out of
joint and I had to carry him to the house and then to the
vet. He couldn't walk for a couple of weeks and then the
legs got better and pretty soon he was sound again. But he
had learned something about rabbits, and he had no use for
them after that. He had a feeling, I think, that a rabbit was

possessed of a secret weapon—a sort of crippling ray. He had been a good fifty feet from that rabbit when the ray hit his back legs.

He was a real Milquetoast. He rarely left our property except for an occasional daring expedition up or down the road, traveling no more than a quarter of a mile and then he'd get frightened at the immensity of the world and come hurrying home. He could do a job of ferocious barking, usually at the wrong people; his most hysterical outbursts were always directed against the delivery truck which brought his meat. Because of his superficial ferocity everyone considered him to be a fine watchdog and said so. Yet he was the world's worst. He'd charge at any and all invaders, barking furiously, so long as I was on the scene to back him up. But we found out later that whenever we were away from the house he had a tendency to crawl off somewhere and hide. A friend arrived one day while we were in New York City, and she went searching for Rufus. Eventually she found him upstairs, under a bed, almost trembling with fright.

He used to go at the laundryman as if he meant to chew the guy to pieces; at the same time he would whine and tremble and cling to my side at a distant rumble of thunder. He didn't seem to know that more dogs have been knocked head over heels by laundrymen than by all the thunderclaps since time began.

❦

My affection for Rufus was a little strange considering the fact that during the years in which I lived in New York City I was a dog-hater. It wasn't a mere distaste for dogs, but a wild and untrammeled bitterness, born of ten thousand meetings with them on the pavements and sidewalks of the city. In later years I realized that my animus wasn't actually directed against the dogs, but rather against the people who owned them, and kept them in the prison of apartments, and put little raincoats and rubber booties on them when they walked them in the rain.

Then I moved to the country and almost immediately, by command of my children, I acquired Rufus. It came about through my reading of a classified ad in the local paper, an ad that was somewhat confusing in its terminology. After studying it for quite a while I concluded that a man named Paul Ganz was giving away cocker spaniels. He lived over in Yorktown, on Baptist Church Road, and when I telephoned him and asked him if it was true, he said it certainly was not true. What the ad meant was that he had some girl dogs that he wanted to stash around at different homes, and they wouldn't really belong to the people who kept them, and occasionally Mr. Ganz would come around with boy dogs, and then something would happen that I never did quite understand, and that's all there was to it, except that there was some mention of puppies. This didn't sound good to me—I said I just wanted to buy a dog, not operate a house of ill fame. So Mr. Ganz drove over one evening, walked into the living room, reached into his coat pocket and pulled out a little black ball and set it on the floor and it promptly peed on the carpet.

A few days later Mr. Ganz sent me a certificate of pedigree—a thing I didn't even have for myself. I didn't like the looks of that pedigree. The dogs involved in the production of Rufus all seemed to be close relatives—first cousins and uncles and aunts and brothers and sisters—and the more I studied the thing the more I thought that I might have an idiot dog on my hands. Rufus was a My Own Brucie cocker. Of his eight great-grandparents, two were My Own

Brucie—the same fellow both times—and one was My Own Miss Brucie, and one was Blackstone Brucie (a dog lawyer?) and one was My Own Old Lace, and one was My Own Clear Doubt. Kinfolks. Close-knit. Clannish. Carrying on under the same roof. Then one of the grandfathers named Pooh-Bah of Angelfear romanced My Own Clear Doubt and to this union was born Rustum of Angelfear and Rustum of Angelfear fell in love with Rebel Beauty of Angelfear (could they have been brother and sister?) and they begat Rufus and Rufus peed on the carpet. His real name was Black Rebel of Mount Kisco but I don't think he ever knew it. He was named Rufus after my friend Rufus Blair of Hollywood. Rufus Blair's daughter, Sandra, when she was about twelve, developed a deep resentment over my having named a dog for her father. She got back at me. One day she came home with an ancient tomcat, and announced to the family that its name was H. Alley Cat.

☺

Any dog that has My Own Brucie for a great-grandfather, twice over, has something to be genuinely proud about, but I'm sure Rufus never gave the matter any thought. He was as common as dirt. He didn't act superior, was opposed to bathing, and ate sticks. It took a long time to get him housebroken. Bluebloods are harder to train in that respect than ordinary dogs; whether this also applies to people is a thing I wouldn't know. After we did get him housebroken it turned out that he was broken to only one house. Whenever he got into a house other than his own, the first thing he looked for was the piano. He seemed to have some prejudice against pianos, or perhaps against music generally. If he couldn't find a piano, he'd use people. One evening when he was still a puppy we had company in, and

[171]

among the guests was a lady of considerable dignity and poise. She was standing by the fireplace with a cocktail in her hand, gassing about Henry James, when her left foot began to feel warmish. She took a sip of her drink and then glanced down at her foot and Rufus was there, just finishing up a great job of work. He had filled her shoe, but there was a saving circumstance. She had on open-toed slippers, and it all ran down and out through the vent in the front. This is the only time I ever saw an application of the practical value of open-toed shoes.

(I wrote a few things about Rufus once in a book, including the incident of the open-toed shoe. Maureen McKernan told me later that there was an 80-year-old priest down-country who, about once every two or three months, would call his assistant and say, "Get the book and read me the part about Rufus and the shoe again." He expressed the wish to meet Rufus before he died, but unhappily I didn't know about it so it never came to pass.)

I must mention that at the same time we got Rufus we acquired two cats and he grew up with them and for a long time I'm sure he believed himself to be a cat. He acquired certain cat habits, the most noteworthy of which was the expert use of his paws. He boxed and slapped with his paws, the way a cat does, and showed a certain dexterity in handling objects with his paws. And he did more licking of his pelt, cat fashion, than any other dog of my acquaintance.

He knew no tricks. He jumped through no hoops. We never tried to get him to heel by saying "heel" to him. That would only have bewildered him because we used the word in another connection at our house. He had an extensive vocabulary, insofar as understanding words was concerned, and we sometimes had to spell out things that we didn't want him to hear. Like most dogs he was daffy about riding in automobiles, and knew the word "car" and when he heard it, he'd get so excited he'd almost swoon. Consequently it was necessary for us sometimes to refer to the c-a-r in his presence. It will not be generally believed, but I take oath that eventually he learned to understand the word when it was spelled out.

3

I did things for him that I shouldn't have done. I often fed him things that were forbidden. I blush to confess that on several occasions I sprinkled Accent on his horse-meat to make it taste better. My attitude toward him was much the same as that of an old man I knew when I was a boy—Old Man Carter. He lived alone with a venerable hound named Jeff and the two of them were inseparable. On Saturday nights Old Man Carter would get loaded on home brew and then he'd take to grieving over the plight of his dog in *merely being a dog.* He'd get to weeping, beerily, and talking to Jeff, and he'd wail, "You're nothin' but a dog—jist a dog—you won't never be nothin' else but a dog—I'd do somethin' about it if I could, but I cain't—Oh God I woosht I could do somethin' about it!"

As I have mentioned, I regarded myself as a dog-hater before Rufus came into my life. And then one evening I realized to the full just how drastically I had changed. We were playing cards in the living room and Rufus was lying at my feet. At the conclusion of the game I stood up and lifted the chair away from the table. It came down on Rufus's paw and being a heavy chair, hurt him. He let out a yell, jumped about three feet across the carpet, and then began crying, looking at me as if I were the most unprincipled villain on earth.

I confess that I went a little out of my head, and got

[173]

panicky. I was *so* distraught, *so* upset about it, *so* sorry. I hadn't done it on purpose. And the feeling that took possession of me was a desperate desire to let him know, somehow, that it was an accident, that I loved him, that I would never be capable of hurting him deliberately. I just *had* to get it across to him . . .

So I whipped the chair.

Another dog? Certainly not. What would I want with a dog? Rufus was not a dog. He was Rufus.

Hallowe'en

Oct. 31–In the beginning our place was known as The Pinnacle, a name I hated from the start. However, deliverymen and taxi drivers were accustomed to using The Pinnacle, so it remained The Pinnacle for the first year and a half of our residence; then the problem was solved on Hallowe'en of 1946.

A report reached me that a gang of Jack Armstrongs, All-American Boys, from the high school in Chappaqua, was planning a raid on my establishment. A neighbor had stopped in at a soda fountain the day before and heard these clean-cut young men, soon to become the spiritual and political leaders of our republic, loudly plotting their expedition. "Let's go up," said their fun-loving leader, his breaking voice reflecting a boyish eagerness, "and rip the bejezus outa that Smith place!"

It was cold that night and grew colder, but I sat on a stone wall in the darkness, a loaded gun beside me and Rufus at my feet. There in the blackness of night I smiled at the fun of it, and thought: After all, boys will be boys, so I won't shoot to kill—I'll just try to mangle them a little, take off an arm or a leg, or place my shot so it will remove only an eye without damaging the brain. At last midnight came, and I waited another fifteen or twenty minutes and then decided that their scheme had miscarried, put the dog in the basement, and went to bed. The following morning, after a refreshing sleep, I found that they had torn down several sections of rail fence, ripped up a decorative hitching post, gouged up the lawn and garden, made off with some ornamental wagon wheels and, glory be, ripped up The Pinnacle sign by its concrete roots and smashed it to bits. As I surveyed the debacle I chuckled understandingly—laughed fit to kill—and went in and phoned a contractor. It cost me around a hundred and fifty dollars to set things straight and I never did replace the signpost. I regret to add, though, that the place was called The Pinnacle for a good while after that. Witty visitors referred to it as The Pinochle. And we had a colored maid who was accustomed to telling the taxi drivers to take her to "The Pimlico."

Election Note

Nov. 1—It is election time. I think it fitting that people be informed about the four versions of The Cut. I have found them listed in an old English almanac, as follows:

(1) The *cut direct* is to stare an acquaintance in the face and pretend not to know him.

(2) The *cut indirect*, to look another way, and pretend not to see him.

(3) The *cut sublime*, to admire the top of some tall edifice or the clouds of heaven till the person cut has passed by.

(4) The *cut infernal*, to stoop and adjust your boots till he has gone past.

Happy electioneering!

Problems of a Butler

Nov. 5–A man called William came to wash the windows before I put up the storm sashes. I got to talking with him and learned that he once served as a butler in several of the big houses around here. "I give it up," he said. "Couldn't take it any more. The thing that killed me was the fact I couldn't never get the people to the table for dinner. I'd announce dinner was ready, and they'd go on standin' around, drinkin' their cocktails, and they'd stand around some more and drink some more, and the food would all get cold, and they still wouldn't come to the table, so I quit. Maybe the younger fellas can put up with it, but I can't. I'd ruther wash windows."

> There are no doubt occasions in history
> when the oppressed are being oppressed be-
> cause they've got it coming to them.
> —*Sayings of Avery*

Etiquette

[There *Is* an Impolite Sex (Not Men)]

Nov. 11—If you ladies of the suburbs will please leave the
room now, we have some things to talk over. I don't want
you around because I'm going to say some harsh things
about you; I'm going to say that you are the impolite sex—
that you are selfish and inconsiderate and that your natural
tendency is to slash and bite. Hey, sister! Didn't I tell you
this is not for you? Quit reading it. Go on to the next story.
Hear me? Go on now!

High police officials of our cities and states periodically
wet the ends of their pencils, loll out their tongues, and
compose solemn pronunciamentos in which they declare
that women are as expert as men at the business of driving
an automobile. Some even say that women are better drivers
than men.

There can be but two possible reasons why a public
functionary, occupying an appointive office, would issue
such a shocking declaration: either he has been goaded into

[177]

doing it by his wife, or the thing that he says is true. I prefer to believe the latter, for the reason that his stated conclusions are usually based on certain driving tests in which females demonstrate a skill at the wheel equal to or even superior to the skill of males.

What these police officials are actually saying is this: women are *capable* of driving as expertly as men. The fact still remains that they don't do it. The fact still remains that the most common phrase heard on our streets and highways is, "Look at that gee dee woman driver!"

There is a monumental discrepancy somewhere, and I think that I have found it. Women are capable drivers, insofar as reflexes and physical adroitness and mental alertness are concerned. But they are sadly lacking in the most important of all qualifications which go to make up a genuinely good driver—consideration for the other fellow. They have none. Absolutely none.

℃

For the last three weeks I have been quietly studying the rude behavior of women drivers, principally on the streets and highways of suburban Westchester County. The inspiration for this bit of anti-social research, which may lead me to an early grave, came on an afternoon when I was parked in the village near my home. There is a depot plaza in this village, and angle parking is the rule. On this particular afternoon I parked and checked my watch and found that I had a half hour to wait for the train I was to meet. I switched on the radio, got a ball game, then slumped myself down in the seat so that I was virtually invisible from the outside.

A woman came up to the car which was parked to the right of mine. The space between my car and her car was less than three feet. She took hold of the door of her car and yanked it open so that it slammed against my fender, denting the chromium trim. I popped up immediately just in time to see her glance into my car. When she saw it was occupied she merely glared bitterly at me, as if *I* had been responsible, slid into the driver's seat, backed out and drove away.

Within a few minutes another car arrived in the vacated space, a car driven by a man. He opened his door carefully, leaning out to make certain it didn't hit my fender. He went into a bank and came out shortly and, once again, handled his door carefully, never once touching my fender.

The third car had a woman driver. Bang! Another dent. Into a store for groceries. Out again. Crash! I think I would have been justified in climbing out of my car, taking a jack handle, and beating dents in her heap from bumper to bumper but, of course, I didn't do it. I did nothing. The prescribed code ordains that the male should never precipitate a dispute in public with a female. He can't win. He has never in history been known to win.

This happened, as I said, three weeks ago. Since then I have put myself in the same situation a dozen times, half hiding myself from view and observing the comings and goings of the cars next to me. Invariably the women have slammed their doors against my car; invariably the men have been considerate and careful.

An idea was beginning to take form and I went on to further observations and it soon became apparent to me why men are forever howling against those gee dee women drivers. A woman at the wheel of an automobile is a bully. She bulls her way into traffic and she bulls her way through it. Watch a woman come out of a side street ahead of you. You have no right-of-way ever, so far as she is concerned.

She gives you a quick contemptuous glance, which says quite clearly, "Look out, jerk—me first!" And she charges in ahead of you. If you have been driving a long time you have learned to expect it, you know she'll do it, and you condition yourself for it to avoid dying like a dog.

A woman will never go out of her way, not eight inches, to facilitate the movement of traffic. She is inclined to behave as if every other automobile in sight is being driven by her personal enemies, while God is her co-pilot. Her own forward progress is all that matters. The sun rises and the sun sets in her muffler. She performs at the wheel as if she were engaged in a race with the stork, or hauling serum, when very likely she is simply on her way to get some technical advice on how to tat a doily.

The traffic problem in our village is as great as it is everywhere else. Our Main Street is narrow and the flow of cars is constant throughout the day. There is no room on that street for double-parking, even for half a minute. One automobile, double-parked while its driver saunters into a drugstore for a firkin of deodorant, can snarl up the street for an hour. Yet I sometimes stand on Main Street and watch the ladies engage in the sport of double-parking. They do it constantly and appear to enjoy doing it. Other drivers blast their horns at them and get in return a cold and hateful glare or an oral invitation to sizzle in hell.

I'm not talking about isolated cases. Women drivers, if anything, are consistent in their rudeness. Watch them backing out of angle-parking places. A man whose car is in such a situation will start backing by inches until he is able to see if anything is coming at him from the rear. If a car is approaching he holds his posititon, waits for it to pass. A woman? Certainly not! She slaps that lever into reverse, tramps on the accelerator and comes charging out

[180]

like a female Dan Tucker, crying, "Git out th' way!" and God preserve anyone, including stray dogs, who happens to be in the path of her backward-leaping buggy. You think I'm exaggerating? Listen—I've been watching it for a long time—long enough to reach the definite conclusion that a woman at the wheel of an automobile has the same consideration for her fellow creatures that a King Cobra has for a mongoose.

☺

Now, let us . . . *the ladies have all gone, haven't they? I don't want them to hear this. It's not that I'm afraid of getting hit on the head with rocks. It's just that . . . well, you know how it is . . .* Let us move now into the broader field of general etiquette. We assume, and rightly I suppose, that books of etiquette are written largely for women. We know, at least, that women are the chief buyers of the etiquette manuals. Should we assume from this that women are the polite members of the race? They actually believe that they are, that the preservation of gentility is altogether in their hands.

It appears to be a fact that women are polite *only toward members of their own circle or clan.* A woman is genteel and well-bred to the person who is a guest in her home, to the members of her club, to her neighbors sometimes, and to people who have been properly introduced to her. But toward the stranger, male or female, her bearing is often that of a savage, a mean, clawing, cantankerous, wild and unpredictable animal. Thus she makes a farce of the whole institution of etiquette which she pretends to worship. Ferocious beasts of the jungle are polite toward their own associates; nobody has to be taught that. The primary function of any code of manners is the promotion

[181]

of amiable relationships between strangers. And that is where the ladies fail.

Have you ever attended a Wednesday matinee in the legitimate theater? Here the audience is at least ninety per cent women, and let us not forget that these are the women who presumably wallow in the writings of Emily Post and all the other arbiters of elegant behavior—these are not scrubwomen and fishwives and grisettes. Yet it would be difficult to find, anywhere on earth, a more barbaric gathering. The flagrant rudeness of a legitimate theater audience on an ordinary evening, with a fair share of men present, is appalling enough; the unalloyed savagery of the matinee audience would frighten a jaguar. The ladies bare their fangs and walk upon each other and perform bruising operations with their elbows. They babble. God how they babble! The last half dozen times I have been to the legitimate theater I have come away with only a hazy notion of what happened on the stage. My two hours have been spent observing the Mummed-up harridans play skin-the-Kilkenny-cat with one another. I have seen them kick each other, and I have seen them seize the straps of their pocket-books and swat. And these are the people who say eyether and nyether and vozz.

One of our great national jokes for many years has been the rampaging fury, the dog-eat-dog deportment, of women attending bargain sales. I, for one, fail to see anything funny in it. To me it is frightening. It might be comical, perhaps, if it were confined to bargain sales, but it is not. The generality of women, whether engaged in clawing the shirtwaists off each other in department stores, or at Wednesday matinees, or driving an automobile, are under some weird sort of compulsion to knock down and trample anyone who gets in their way. Compare their behavior with that of a crowd that is overwhelmingly male—a crowd, say, at Madison Square Garden on fight night. The men walk in and take their seats and watch the show and then get up and walk out. They are orderly about it and considerate of one another, and if one man treads on the feet of another in getting to his seat, there is no exchange of nasty, hate-laden glares, as is the case with women in the same circumstances, but polite apology and equally polite forgiveness.

If the ladies overheard me just now, they'd surely feel that at last they have me by the short hairs. They know from the evidence on their television screens that fist-fights are not uncommon among the customers at boxing shows. I concede the point and suggest that we subpoena the cops and the ushers who work the boxing arenas. Those fights among spectators, they will testify, are not ordinarily engendered by partisan feelings for individual boxers in the ring. The cops and the ushers say that nine times out of ten they are brought about by dames. A male customer seated in the vicinity of a lady permits his emotions to get so far out of hand that he utters a loud profanity. Whereupon the lady turns to her escort and says: "Pilsbury, I have been insulted. Get up on your feet right this minute and clout that scum!" And Pilsbury gets up and clouts, and the scum clouts back, and if Pilsbury gets his skull cracked he has it coming for ever bringing the dame there in the first place.

It happens that some of my best friends are women, so I arrive with reluctance at the conclusion that the genteel gender is the masculine. A gentleman who helps organize golf tournaments recently told me that when the contestants are male the entire operation comes off smoothly and the utmost decorum prevails; in a woman's tournament the sheer bitchery of the gals, in such small matters as the conceding of putts, provides a spectacle that would curdle the mind of a psychiatrist. There is no place on earth more pleasant and peaceable than the bar which caters exclusively to men; by the same token a cocktail lounge loaded with females is a dangerous and disorderly house. Go into a grocery store or meat market and watch the women lie about who's next; such brawling is never encountered in a barber shop. Stand in line at a . . .

What's that? They're coming back . . . the ladies? Okay. Don't tell them what I've been saying. No sense starting a war, wrecking the furniture. I'm not afraid of them, understand, it's just that . . . well, you know. Anyway, I think they ought to be grateful—didn't I come right out flat-footed and say they're capable of driving an automobile as expertly as men?

———◆———

Jack Wheeler's Good Deed

Nov. 16–Jack Wheeler once had a tenant farmer on his place, a man of intelligence but lacking a formal education. Mr. Wheeler used to think it was a shame that this man, with his good mind, had never had an opportunity to study.

"One day," says Mr. Wheeler, "I decided that I would try to introduce him to some good books. I felt certain that if this man had a chance to read the classics, he'd get more out of them than most of us . . ."

So on a November day about a year ago, Mr. Wheeler

took a copy of Plato from his shelves and walked down to the house occupied by the tenant farmer and after discussing various agricultural matters, he casually handed the book to the man and suggested that he might find it interesting.

Weeks passed, and then Mr. Wheeler saw his farmer again. Nothing was said about Plato so finally Mr. Wheeler asked the man if he had read the book.

"Sure did," said the farmer. "Read it all the way through and you know something—that fella thinks the same way I do."

———◆◆———

Jigsaw Puzzle

Nov. 20—Our house was in a neat condition when we moved in, but in the quarters above the garage I found a cardboard box with some assorted junk in it. Included among this rubbish were some pieces of a jigsaw puzzle. I dug them all out and preserved them and one day set up a bridge table and started trying to piece them together. It soon became apparent that most of the pieces were missing, but they began turning up. I found half a dozen in the garage. A few more were half buried under the shrubbery beside the kitchen door. Soon I had everyone searching for them, and I began thinking that this was the way a jigsaw puzzle should be organized, and a pattern began to evolve on the bridge table. I'd fuss with the thing for a while and then go out and wander around in the fields, eyes on the ground, and maybe at the foot of a tree or beside a boulder I'd find another piece, and hurry back with it and try to fit it in. Seemingly a child, or maybe even a dog, had carried the fragments all over the property. Carpenters and painters and masons who worked for us during those early weeks got instructions from me to look for pieces of a jigsaw puzzle and not to throw them away. They found some in the bunkhouse down in the woods, and more out by the incinerator, and a couple turned up when I spaded the garden. I never did, of course, get all of them, or nearly all of them, but from what I had, I figured out that the picture when completed would have shown an ape biting another ape.

No ball game is ever much good unless the people involved hate each other.

—*Sayings of Avery*

Sociology

[The Pinhole Audience]

Nov. 24—Today is Thanksgiving, and this afternoon Cornell played Pennsylvania before a crowd of some 75,000 at Philadelphia. For the sole reason that my son was a graduate of Cornell I was interested in the game. Not enough to attend it in the flesh with my heir, but I did stay home and watch it on television.

My wife has no interest in the sporting life, yet the moment the pre-game shennanigans began, she came in and planted herself in front of the screen and stayed with it to the end. She doesn't know how the game came out; she doesn't know the names of any of the players who starred. It may be that she doesn't even know that Cornell's opponents were from the University of Pennsylvania. She spent the whole afternoon trying to get a TV glimpse of her boy.

When the cameras were trained on the playing field she stared blankly at the screen; but when there were occasional shots of the crowded stands, she would leap forward, get her face within two feet of the picture, and start

[187]

searching. One camera would shoot across the field to the stands on the far side—producing little more than a blur—and she'd be up there, trying to locate her son in that blur.

It was another November afternoon, about a year ago, that I think that I first became aware of the Pinhole Audience in television, composed of people who have no interest whatever in the subject matter portrayed on the screen. They are looking for, or at, somebody they know, or somebody their friends know. They concentrate all their attention on one human being, or even on one inanimate object; that person or that object is seen as through an optometrist's pinhole disc.

So far as I know, the people who run television—the advertising agencies and the executives of the several stations and networks—have never given a moment's consideration to this special audience. Yet I am convinced that it runs into the tens of thousands. And assuming that it is an important and sizeable segment of the total TV audience, it should be granted some attention. I don't know exactly what the television people can do by way of serving this Pinhole Audience; I don't know how the advertising agencies might figure out a way to address a portion of their message to these people. I do know that the advertising agencies have figured out a great many things that I never thought could be figured out, so maybe they'll come up with something. Meanwhile, I have done a bit of ground-work for them.

I didn't really decide on conducting my survey until after I was invited one evening to the home of a neighbor who had several guests out from the city. After dinner one of these guests, a robust lady with a jutting chin, marched up to the television set, turned it on, and settled into a chair directly in front of the screen. This struck me as unseemly conduct. A point of mid-century etiquette was involved—nobody, including the host, turns on TV unless there is an overwhelming clamor for it. I glanced at my host, raising my eyebrows, and he whispered: "It's all right. She's getting the ball game. She's Mrs. George Piggott." I recognized the name at once (as is my custom I had been addressing her as Mrs. Blodgett all through dinner). She was the consort of George Piggott, the baseball umpire.

Mrs. George Piggott behaved in much the same manner as my wife had behaved while watching the Cornell-Penn game. A home run stirred no emotion within her breast; a sparkling catch by an outfielder wrought no display of approval or disapproval. Her eye was on George Piggott, who was back of the plate. As you probably know, George Piggott has a talent for embroilment with players and managers, and Mr. Piggott is not popular with many of the fans. They boo him, and they booed him in this particular game. It was a strange experience, sitting there and hearing the waves of boos coming from the stands, and watching the wife of the man against whom they were directed.

The moment the abuse of her husband began, she'd stiffen in her chair. "Booooooooooo!" she'd bray at the top of her voice. "Booooooooooo yourselves, ya bums ya!" And then when the camera swung around to show the indignant crowd, she'd place her tongue between her lips and give them the noise that has often been described as unprintable.

When the ball game was over we sat back and she talked a bit about her husband's performance, and the villainy of those ballplayers who had given him an argument, and especially of the paying customers, whom she described as no better than morons. "They hadn't oughta be allowed inside ball-yards," she said. "Every last one of them oughta be barred."

Mrs. George Piggott's performance set me to thinking about the Pinhole Audience and led eventually to the survey I have just completed. I have sought out members of this special audience and interviewed them, and I am now prepared to publish my findings. Both the advertising and the television professions are welcome to employ these findings as they see fit. Limitations of space do not permit my publishing all of the case histories I have collected; I'm only presenting a sort of cross-section of the survey results. The following individuals, then, are representative of the whole:

POMEROY MEAD. Mr. Mead is a plumber, resident in Queens. He lives two doors from Googy Appleby, the fight handler, and has known Mr. Appleby personally for three years. Mr. Mead never misses a fight telecast when Googy Appleby is working. Mr. Mead cares nothing about the fighters; he doesn't give a hoot who wins. He has eyes only for Googy Appleby and he is unhappy when the camera is away from Mr. Appleby's zone of endeavor. When the camera *does* move to the corner where Mr. Appleby is working over his fighter between rounds, Mr. Mead is inclined to cry out, "Lookit ole Googy! Good ole Googy!" And quite often when the camera goes to the opposite corner Mr. Mead grows indignant and addresses abusive remarks toward the camera crew, yelling, "Git that camera over'n th' other cawner, ya creeps!" Mr. Mead cannot name any world's champion fighter in any of the several classes.

MISS DAPHNE WAGGIN. Miss Waggin is a secretary, age twenty-five. When she was in grade school in North Carolina she was a classmate of Fuff Forenzo, now a relief pitcher. Miss Waggin tunes in all night games and all weekend games in which Fuff Forenzo might possibly pitch. He isn't called on often but he is usually in the bull pen, and during each game there are customarily four or five quick camera shots of the bull pen and Miss Waggin fancies she can pick her old schoolmate out of the group. On those days when Fuff Forenzo does come in to pitch, Miss Waggin is beside herself. "Just think," she usually exclaims as Fuff strides in from the bull pen, "me and him went to school together. Come on Fuff!"

THOMAS YERBE. Mr. Yerbe is a grocer, age forty-seven. He is the uncle of Cool Twining, trombone player in the studio band which plays during the variety show presided over by Hominy Jones, the comedian. Mr. Yerbe never misses the Hominy Jones show, even though the jokes whiz past him without touching him. The fact is, he doesn't even hear them. His ear is tuned for one sound—the cool honking of Cool Twining's sliphorn. On rare occasions he gets a glimpse of his nephew but usually he has to content himself with listening for the sound of his trombone. When he does hear it, he cries out, "There he is! Listen to 'im go! Wowie!"

MRS. PETE WARFEL. Mrs. Warfel is the wife of the man who has charge of cutting the grass in the infield at Belmont Park. The Warfels have four children and a host of cousins. When the races at Belmont are being televised you may be certain the Warfel set is turned on and all available members of the clan are in front of it. They are indifferent about the horses. They lean forward and stare at the infield. Sometimes they comment favorably about the job Pop has done but they can be critical, too. Mrs. Warfel has, on occasion, said: "Well, now, I don't know. Look over there on the left, top of the picksha. Looks just a little ragged, don't you think?"

JAKE. No last name. French hairdresser. M. Jake dresses the hair of Miss Carol Grope, up-and-coming ballad singer, who croons one number each week on the *I'll Buy That* variety show. M. Jake tunes in this show regularly and frets until Miss Grope appears, and then exclaims Frenchily over the marvel of her hair. He doesn't notice her singing, for he is concentrating all his attention on the waves he installed. He sometimes cries out: "Look at ze hair! Zat girl deserves to have her own show!"

CYRIL GRUNTLEY. Tobacconist. Mr. Gruntley has a speaking acquaintance with Ed Fedder, a forecaster with the United States Weather Bureau. Mr. Gruntley, because of this acquaintanceship, has become keenly interested in weather. Each evening he tunes in Cad Millholland's weather program and when Mr. Millholland begins a semi-technical discourse on the weather map, Mr. Gruntley snorts. "Listen to the dumbell!" he says to Mrs. Gruntley. "Talks like he knows what he's talkin' about. Ed Fedder gave him all the datter. The dumbell don't know an occluded front from a Bermuda high!"

MRS. TEET McNELLIS. Mother of four. Her husband is a member of the ground crew at Yankee Stadium. Mrs. McNellis and her children are among the few people in the metropolitan area who consistently pray for rain before and during a ball game, who suffer deep pangs when a game is progressing under cloudless skies. Only if it rains do they stand a chance of getting a glimpse of Teet McNellis as he helps unroll the covering for the infield.

SPOOKY. A cocker spaniel. Member of the Vincent Goff household in suburban New Jersey. Several years ago Spooky had the honor to romp for a full thirty minutes with a dachshund named Ballyhoopin Gaylord of Soapstone during a visit to a public park. Since that memorable day Ballyhoopin Gaylord of Soapstone has been entered each year in the dog show at Madison Square Garden and during the telecasts of this event, the Goffs gather before their screen, with Spooky, and watch intently for the appearance of the aristocratic dachshund. When he does come in view, even in a group of dogs, there are cries of delight from the Goffs, and Spooky is seized and lifted to the screen. One Goff holds him, another twists his head toward the screen, and the others cry: "Look, Spooky! There he is! You played with him! Remember? Oh, darn it, come on and *look!*" Unbiased and cynical observers of this scene believe that Spooky has never once recognized his old friend.

MRS. SOPHIE SAWTERN. Housewife. Mrs. Sawtern is the mother of Herman Sawtern, age sixteen, who works at Television Playhouse No. 23. It is from this Television Playhouse that the weekly dramatic program, *Let's See a Show*, emanates. Herman's job is to provide the actors and other members of the company with coffee and sandwiches, running the provender in from a delicatessen two blocks away. He carries coffee and sandwiches all week during rehearsals, and sometimes runs other errands. On the evening *Let's See a Show* is presented to the public, Mrs. Sawtern telephones her friends and neighbors and says, "Herman's play is on tonight. Come on over and watch." Usually there are half a dozen guests present when Herman's play goes on. This audience never quite follows the story line, being more interested in Mrs. Sawtern's comments on the various performers. "Herman says," she'll announce, "that *she* keeps a bottle of gin in her dressing room and is spiffed about three-fourths of the time." Or, "Look at him! Oh, he's handsome enough, but Herman says all the others hate him because he eats scenery or some such thing. And he's simply *terrible* to his wife." The friends and neighbors exclaim over these revelations and try their best to make complimentary remarks about Herman's work, such as, "Well, one thing you can say, they don't look *hungry!*"

J. Lissom Forwood. Dentist. Mr. Forwood's brother, Ferd Forwood, works on the murder show, *Soft-Boiled Detective*. He appears, or a part of him appears, only at the very beginning of the show, during the Skum soap commerical. It is Ferd Forwood's hand which comes dramatically into view holding a bar of Skum. The rest of him is never seen. As the Forwood hand fades from view, Dr. Forwood sometimes turns to Mrs. Forwood and says, "Well, what do you think?" And she responds, "Good show!" Whereupon they turn the set off and go to bed.

These ten are sufficient to show the nature and extent of the Pinhole Audience.

Cockarouse Cocktimus

Nov. 29–I just came across another reference to Cockarouse Cocktimus, who was an Indian chief who lived in the forest of North Westchester at the time the white man came to take over the county. He was boss of the Indians in the neighborhood of Katonah and Mount Kisco. I have run across his name in the books two or three times, but in each instance the historian has bypassed him quickly, noting only that he was one of the chiefs who signed a paper conveying land to the whites, and then letting him disappear into the mist of time. We are not even told whether he signed his full name or, as in the case of most Indians, used an X. Apparently the exploits of Cockarouse Cocktimus are lost to history. This paragraph is the longest mention he has ever had in print. I wish I could write more about him, but I can't. Anybody named Cockarouse Cocktimus, and especially an Indian named Cockarouse Cocktimus, is entitled to more than a passing glance in the chronicle of mankind.

WINTER

———— ✦ ————

On Monday mornings I am dedicated to the
proposition that all men are created jerks.
                                    —Sayings of Avery

The Seven Thirty-six

[Not Commuting Is No Fun]

December 3—Some things have been said by my wife and
others about my staying home day in and day out, year
upon bitter year. The truth is, occasionally I set the alarm
clock for six-thirty, get out of bed, shave and shower, bolt
down some breakfast and catch the 7:36 for New York
City. I do it sometimes when I have no substantial reason
for going to the city. If the regular commuters on the 7:36
knew about it they would conclude that, as the English
put it, my head wants seeing to. The fact seems to be that
I have become a little envious of those other commuters—
the thousand or so men of my general neighborhood who
ride the trains to and from New York every weekday in
the year. Why should they have all the fun?

My envy of the commuter is not predicated on any
such thing as domestic imprisonment. I've simply arrived
at the conclusion that not commuting is no fun. The commuter leads a life of adventure and excitement as compared
to my way of life. Going to work, for me, consists in walk-

ing slowly across a thirty-foot breezeway. I see nobody, except perhaps an occasional chipmunk. I hear nothing, except perhaps an occasional distant rumble of a commuter train banging along down the valley toward Chappaqua. Yet the commuter is the man who complains bitterly that his method of going to work is dull and dreary and even disgusting. He doesn't know when he's well off. And for all his griping, he doesn't really believe what he says about commuting. Go out and find a man who has been commuting for years and who has through disability or retirement, stopped doing it. He professes publicly that he is now happy and contented, but secretly he misses the old routine and yearns to get back on the 7:36 or the 8:01. He feels much the same way a man might feel when he has been expelled from his club.

There lies the answer. The commuter car is a club. A train with eight cars is a train composed of eight rolling men's clubs. True, there are occasional female invasions, but the clubs really belong to the men. And they are perhaps the most remarkable fraternal groups on earth. They have an unwritten but well-defined code of conduct and they require adherence to it. Without the use of blackballs or ballots they are accustomed to expel any member who violates that code and shows no sign of repentance.

The same men customarily occupy the same car every morning and again in the evening. Most of them prefer to occupy the same seats. They are together then for approximately two hours and a half every weekday. They have a strong fraternal feeling even though, in many cases, they don't know each other's names and don't want to know them.

℃

In joining the commuters occasionally, I have not made the mistake of trying to talk to them on the train, but I have sought out a number of them on week-ends and questioned them about the workings of the Commuter Code. This code serves as the basis for relationships that are, in a peculiar way, both intimate and remote. Among its major clauses are the following:

CLASS DISTINCTION

Only two classes are recognized: those who ride in the smoking cars and those who ride elsewhere. The smoking car is primarily for rowdy people and the code does not apply to them. They are the talkers, the clowns, the card players, and the psychological misfits. They are not wanted in the cars where the dignity of man prevails and they know it, and as a general thing they stay in their proper place.

CONVERSATION

All but forbidden. If there is any talk at all it should be limited to monosyllables. Two men may occupy the same seat every morning for ten years. They bury their faces in their newspapers and keep quiet. They never discuss the news, no matter how important it may be. The only time conversation is permitted is during extremes of weather, e.g., the morning after a violent blizzard. A man is then allowed to say, as succinctly as possible, that the thermometer on his back porch read six below when he got up, that he skidded badly coming down Captain Merritt's hill, that seven cars were stalled on the Millwood Road and that school's been cancelled for the day. His seatmate is permitted to outline his own harrowing experiences reaching the station and to compare this storm with the storm of seven years ago. Then the first man is expected to say, "Eight years ago, not seven." After that they busy themselves with their newspapers. Discussion closed. If one or the other carries on too long there is an immemorial gesture employed to remind him that he is overstepping the bounds of decency. His seatmate simply opens his newspaper and snaps it violently three or four times. That means shut up.

OUTSIDE SOCIAL CONTACTS

Disapproved. These same two men who spend twelve and a half hours together each week may encounter each other in the local supermarket or drug store or tavern. They don't speak. It is permitted for one to nod pleasantly in recognition, although some commuters regard even nodding as presumptuous. There is, however, no rigid law that says commuters may not become friends and visit back and forth on week-ends, but such cases are rare and probably involve men who work in the same office or who married sisters. Where they do develop, the other commuters regard these alliances as a sign of weak character on the part of both principals, who lose caste and are sometimes frowned at.

YACKING

Two men who become friendly off the train are likely to become *talkers* on the train. They may ignore their newspapers altogether and spend the entire journey talking about their wives, their children, their golf, their barbecue sauce, or even the State of the Nation. Such men usually talk in loud tones because of the train noises. They are tolerated for a brief while. They draw scowls and sometimes newspapers will be snapping vigorously all up and down the aisle in protest against their rude behavior. If they don't take the hint, the morning will come when they get the warning that usually precedes expulsion. From somewhere in the car, concealed behind a newspaper, an angry voice will sound: "Write notes!" If they are wise men they will take up their newspapers and cease their gabble.

EXPULSION

This is achieved not through voting, not through committee action, but through the exercise of community scorn. A member who has violated any part of the code and shown no sign of remorse learns of his expulsion through the attitudes of other members. They don't look at him. On station platforms they walk away from him. Whenever their eyes do happen to meet his, they glower. When he starts to take his regular seat in the train the other occupant says gruffly: "I'm holding this for a party." He knows that the time has come for him to pick up his brief case and depart. He joins another club—moves to another car. But he is not persecuted further; his sins don't follow him into his new affiliation. Word of his disgrace is never passed from car to car and he is permitted to establish himself under new conditions to the best of his ability. It is assumed that he has learned his lesson. If he hasn't, he will be expelled ultimately from other groups and end up with the raffish element in the smoking car.

CHICKEN

Whenever the train comes to a shuddering halt and the conductors and brakemen start racing through the cars and yanking at cords, no member is to show the slightest evidence of concern. It is forbidden even to raise one's eyes from the newspaper. If a member should lose his composure so completely that he asks a brakeman or conductor what has happened, his disgrace is complete and his expulsion immediate.

DELAYS

If mechanical trouble keeps the train standing still for more than four minutes, the membership is permitted to display emotion. Not alarm, however. At the end of four minutes it is legal for the members to begin grumbling. This grumbling must follow a definite pattern and must be directed against the railroad company, with special reference to the poor quality of its rolling stock and the depravity of its train crews. If the delay lasts as much as *seven* minutes, then louder and more forceful denunciation is in order and the use of selected profanity is allowed.

TRANSIENTS

The occasional transient who invades the club, dislocating its tranquillity merely by his presence, has certain unalienable rights and they must be respected. That is, provided his attitude is correct. The correct attitude for a transient is for him to preserve a meek demeanor, to hang his head slightly and to keep his eyes lowered in humility and in the knowledge that he really has no business here.

DRUNKS

A fairly familiar sight on the outbound commuter train is the man who has lingered overlong at bar. He usually swings open the door at the head-end of the car and stands there swaying, surveying the scene with a glittering eye. He may burst into raucous song, or he may burst into a tirade against the occupants of the car, calling them a bunch of slobs and stuffed shirts and even worse; or he may even be boiling over with affection—inclined to lurch down the aisle bestowing clumsy embraces and damp kisses on various members. The club's attitude toward him depends entirely on his status. If he is a transient, or if he belongs in another car, he is scorned and denounced. Shouts may come from behind newspapers up and down the car's length, shouts such as, "Throw the bum out the window!" or "Will somebody kindly strangle him?" On the other hand, if he happens to be a member of the club, a regular occupant of the car and in good standing, a certain tolerance is granted him. The members merely smile wryly and say, "He's feeling a little good."

WOMEN

The loveliest female creature on earth can walk into a commuter car and take a seat without creating the slightest stir. I have this on the authority of half a dozen male commuters. It's true that they stated the proposition in the presence of their wives, but they are honorable men and I don't doubt them. They say that one of the strictest rules in the code demands that a pretty girl go unnoticed, or that she be looked upon as if she were constructed of knotty pine. She must never be ogled.

Through personal investigation I have found that this rule is slightly flexible. It applies only inside the railroad car (assuming that it applies at all). The code changes radically the moment the young lady's feet hit the station platform. A man who has studiously ignored her for over an hour, during which time she may have been occupying the seat beside him, is permitted to follow her down the station platform, offer to smash her baggage, offer to give her a lift in his car, offer her a stick of gum, offer her anything.

THE WOLF

There is always at least one man on every train who violates the above rule concerning females. He is known, to be sure, as The Wolf, and he belongs in no particular car and is therefore immune to punishment. His tactics are not precisely those of the ordinary masher. He walks from car to car until he sights a pretty girl alone in a seat. Having spotted the prey, he pretends to be studying his newspaper as he moves along the aisle and then suddenly he glances at the vacant seat beside her and quickly lowers himself into it. There may be a dozen other vacant seats in the car, but he'll act as if this were the only one. Entirely an accident that fate has thrown him into physical proximity with this ravishing creature. He believes that his performance is one of masterful subtlety and that nobody has noticed it. Everybody has noticed it. Everybody notices it every day. The Wolf is looked upon as a sick man, out of balance mentally. He is considered to be sick for the reason that he never attempts to talk to the girl. It is obvious from his conduct that he believes the day will come when one of these beautiful young women will turn and look at him and decide he is what she has been looking for and perhaps even grasp him and claim him as her own. Available statistics show that this has not yet happened.

CARD PLAYERS

These are the Jukes and the Kallikaks of the commuter world.

As a general rule they have been exiled to the smoking car where eccentric conduct of any nature is permitted. They are inclined to be a noisy lot and even in the smoking cars the cry of "Pipe down!" has sometimes sounded.

They have their own code, which revolves around the matter of kibitzer seniority. The same four players get on the same car every morning and occupy the same car coming home at night. The brakeman is under contract to set up their private casino, furnishing the lapboard and cards, for which he is paid a daily fee. There are usually two official kibitzers, sometimes three, and they are important to the organization of the game. Let us suppose that four men who have been playing in the same bridge game for years get on the train at Grand Central. They begin playing at once. One of the players has to get off at Hawthorne station, while the other three continue to Brewster. When the train reaches the Hawthorne station, Kibitzer Number One comes into his glory. He pops into the vacated seat and takes over the hand. He is always present, ready to sit in if an emergency develops, such as a player missing the train, or being compelled by his wife to go on vacation, or getting sick. If a regular player dies, or is transferred to another city, or has his office hours changed, then Number One moves in as a permanent player. Kibitzer Number Two is promoted to Number One, and a new man is appointed to serve as Number Two. The card players, as mentioned, are rowdy and noisy. They are held in contempt by the conservative occupants of the other cars. Yet there are some observers who say that they have more fun than anybody else on the train.

Thus a basic portion of the code that governs the commuter. I hope you see, as I see, that it is an important and invigorating phase of modern American living. And why I am getting sick and tired of staying home all the time and missing all that fun.

Anybody know of a job I could get in the city? Just any old kind of a job—so long as the hours are regular.

Civic Research

December 5–My neighbor Avery just came over to tell me about a small experiment he conducted a couple of days ago. (He doesn't have much to do when winter sets in.) His house sits on a knoll, above the town highway. In the morning around ten o'clock he took a brick down, placed it on the road in a position which made it necessary for a car to swerve to avoid hitting it. Then Avery concealed himself up near his house, sitting in a chair back of some shrubbery. He watched from ten in the morning until two-thirty in the afternoon. Around two-thirty an oil delivery truck stopped and the driver got out and removed the brick from the road. Avery said that nine-tenths of the drivers who went around the brick were women. He had conducted the experiment to prove a point. The women of our neighborhood, almost all of them, participate like crazy in all manner of civic things. They form committees and conduct drives and put on charity affairs. They are on the go constantly with these things. "But," said Avery, "they really haven't got a single god damned spark of civic consciousness in them. If they did have, they'd have stopped and taken that brick out of the road."

Some performers on television appear to be horrible people, but when you finally get to know them in person, they turn out to be even worse.

–Sayings of Avery

Weights and Measures

[How to Estimate Distance]

December 10–When I went over to see Williams this afternoon I wasn't able to find his house, so I drove back to the village and got him on the phone.

"You pass that tennis court," he said, "and then go about two hundred yards and you'll see my driveway on the left."

"Two hundred yards," I murmured to myself. "That's two football fields."

"What's that you said?" his voice came over the phone.

"Two football fields," I repeated. "I'll explain it when I get there."

And I did. I told him that I have always been invincibly stupid when it comes to estimating distances, whether they be in inches, feet, yards, rods, furlongs, miles, light years or parsecs.

"The only time I'm pretty sure of my ground," I said, "is when I have something, like say a football field, to fasten in my mind. When I have a distance that somebody has mentioned to me, and it is a certain number of yards in length, then I can apply the football field, lay it down on the ground, so to speak, and then I visualize this other . . ."

"Hold it," Williams interrupted. "I think you've lost me."

"What I mean," I said, "is that a football field is a hundred yards; if something else is two hundred yards long, then I know it is two football fields laid end to end."

Williams said well he'd be darned, he was exactly the same way. He is unerring, he said, on anything that is fifty feet long.

"When I was a kid," he explained, "I won a medal at a rifle meet shooting at a target fifty feet away. To this day I can measure off fifty feet without a tape and hit it within an inch or two. All other distances have me baffled. That is, except ninety feet. I've learned that one from my son."

Williams Junior is a baseball addict and is acutely conscious of the fact that it's ninety feet from home plate to first base. Around the Williams property, as well as on vacation trips, the boy is forever looking for something that is ninety feet away, so he can say that it is. "That stump over there with the bird on it," he'll announce with great authority, "is almost exactly ninety feet from us."

Williams said that since we were both dumb on distances, it ought to be possible for us to broaden the football-field and bird-on-a-stump system. For one thing, we are living in a focusing era and it is necessary to judge distances in order to take clear photographs. In fact, distance-estimating is a kind of skill that comes in handy in many pursuits, such as parallel parking, thinking about a new carpet for the living room, criticizing your neighbor's crummy swimming pool, locating cocktail parties in the country, testifying about powder burns, and so on.

It may readily be seen that the world of sports, being fraught with distances of many kinds and varieties, can provide us with certain rule of thumb techniques (the thumb itself is no good any more except in estimating the length of pickles). Golfers are always good at judging distances, with special reference to four and one-quarter inches, the legal diameter of the hole into which the ball, with a diameter of only 1.680 inches, so seldom seems to fit. I once knew a dedicated horseplayer who claimed he was perfect at judging 770 yards (although he rarely could find any practical use for this talent). That is the distance of the longest home stretch in the world, at Aqueduct. My friend explained that all the frenzy and hysteria in the sport of kings, and it is considerable, is concentrated in that final stretch run. "I could run it myself blindfolded," he said, "and know exactly when I hit the finish line."

As against the slapdash comparison technique, I have no faith in the business of "pacing off" yardage. During the last dozen years I've had extensive dealings with a contracting firm, made up of two partners. One partner is a man scarcely over five feet tall. The other is six feet three. I have watched both of them pace off distances on my own property, and it makes me nervous. The tall partner believes that his stride is exactly one yard, but I'm certain that it's more. The short partner is conscious of the fact that his legs are short and so *he* does *his* pacing in little hops and leaps, so that he looks like a ballet dancer in a business suit. I wouldn't trust him to pace off a hog wallow. These two men, pacing one after the other, supervised the building of my long driveway. On the one hand it came out to be 158 yards long and on the other, 172. Then I measured it with a tape and found it to be 165 yards. If I had taken the ballet dancer's estimate, my driveway would have run clear across the road and through Dr. Heinemann's gate.

On the theory that other people have trouble estimating distances I have worked out a small table of helpful suggestions.

THREE FEET: If you are of average height you may be surprised to learn that your leg is just about three feet, or one yard, long. So if you need to estimate three feet, kick your leg straight out in front of you and hold it there and look at it.

NINE FEET: Not long ago in Honolulu I met the proprietor of a cemetery (I met him socially) and for some reason we got to talking about distances and he said he was very good at nine feet, which is the required length of a grave in Hawaii. He said it is ten feet on the mainland.

TEN FEET: See nine feet.

THIRTEEN FEET: Think of two Gary Coopers lying end to end, both wearing cowboy boots. This same system can be used in estimating six and a half feet, with only one Cooper.

FIFTEEN FEET: At the age of five I fell into a freshly dug cistern and I can remember that everyone made a big thing out of the fact that it was "fifteen-foot" deep. That distance is ineradicably and traumatically engraved on my mind. The trouble is, however, it is a vertical distance and somehow I can't seem to bend it over and flatten it out against the ground. It will come in handy, however, if I am ever fifteen feet up a telegraph pole and want to notify people how far up a telegraph pole I am.

TWENTY-FIVE FEET: I always get my wife to estimate this one for me. It is the precise distance the man skidded before crashing into her car that day on the Saw Mill River Parkway. The police measured the skid marks and she says she now knows twenty-five feet better than she knows her own children. If you happen to witness an automobile accident in which someone has skidded, worm your way in close and observe the measurement of the tire marks. It's better, of course, to be *in* the accident.

SEVENTEEN FEET: Measure the overall length of your automobile. It may turn out to be seventeen feet. Memorize that length by walking from bumper to bumper, back and forth, reciting over and over, "Seventeen feet, seventeen feet, seventeen feet." Don't be embarrassed if a neighbor comes along and catches you at it. Simply tell him that you are rehearsing a part in an amateur theatrical production, a detective story.

SIXTY FEET: Recently the skipper of an auxiliary ketch asked me to sign on as a member of his crew and sail with him to Tahiti. I wanted to do it and spent an entire afternoon pacing that little vessel from stem to stern, trying to make up my mind. I compared its size to that of a huge ocean liner that had recently docked with a cargo of seasick passengers and shattered furniture. I learned sixty feet so well that I'll always know it but as far as the Tahitian voyage was concerned, I chickened out. A full-grown chicken is eleven inches long, if you want to remember eleven inches.

NINETEEN MILES: It is a good thing to know this distance in case there is a town or a tavern nineteen miles from where you live, and you want to tell your neighbors how far they'll have to go to get there. The best way to learn to estimate nineteen miles is to grease up and swim the English Channel. An easier method is to go to that tavern.

NINETY-THREE MILLION MILES: We now have all kinds of astronomical distances to worry about from day to day, and we might as well try to cope with them. It's almost frightening to realize that the moonshooters, employing the technique of a hunter leading a duck, aim their rockets at a point about 137,000 miles ahead of their moving target. I heard a man say so. Now there is talk of shooting something at the sun. The mean distance from the earth to the sun is 93,000,000 miles. That's a mean distance to estimate, but it can be done. The moon is only 239,000 miles from the earth and we have come to know that distance pretty intimately. Thus it becomes a simple matter to visualize the distance from Cape Canaveral to the sun. The way it figures out, it is 390 times as far to the sun as it is to the moon. Get the moon distance (239,000 miles, give or take a yard) firmly fixed in your mind and then lay it out 390 times (the way I do it with football fields) and when you've got it laid out end to end 390 times, you'll have the distance to the sun just as solidly fixed in your mind. That is, *you'll* have it. I don't think I will, because I'm going back to the old-fashioned ways, back to that bird on the stump.

A Winter's Tale

December 13–We have had some cold weather and it has reminded Avery that he never told me about his war record. He was in the army in World War I and fought his way up to private first class.

"I'm a man," said Avery, "who has always liked to sleep late. I had a sergeant who thought I ought to get up. We were always having arguments about it. One morning everybody else was up and had gone and I was still asleep. This sergeant walked in and took hold of the blankets and jerked them off of me. He should have known that was a dangerous thing to do. An Avery would never allow such a thing to happen. I sprang over the foot of the bed and knocked him down and when he got up I knocked him clear down the wooden stairs. So when he came to, he went to the lieutenant and told him what happened, and wanted to know what they ought to do to me. The lieutenant said, 'Well, bring me the rules of court martial and we'll see how many things we can get the bastard on.' I did a good job of talking and got out of it pretty well; they only busted me to buck private."

———◆◆———

Gumperson's Law

December 14–There is a pseudoscientific statute called Gumperson's Law which I sometimes feel was passed solely for me. It is a law dealing with the innate animosity of inanimate objects. I have known about it for years; it was first promulgated under its present name in the magazine *Changing Times* which defined its operation as follows: The outcome of a given desired probability will be inverse to the degree of desirability. Thus, all the vacant parking places are on the other side of the street. Thus, you can use two boxes of matches and a whole edition of the Sunday paper without being able to start a fire under the dry logs in your fireplace, but if you throw a burnt match out the window of the car you are almost certain to start a forest fire.

I have long been intimately acquainted with Gumperson's Law for I live under it. I am getting so I hate to see Sunday come around, because it is always on that day I get a raging toothache—when all the dentists are golfing. I dislike going to the garage with a rattle in my car, because the moment the mechanic begins his inspection, that rattle will vanish. If one of my friends is going to be on television, and urges me to watch his performance, I grow apprehensive at once, knowing that my set will break down the moment the show goes on the air. I do not know Dr. Gumperson, but I have a strong feeling that somehow he has heard about me.

[213]

> I may get as mad as hell at someone on occa-
> sion, but this you can depend on—I always
> hold a grudge.
>
> —*Sayings of Avery*

Social Season

[The Problem of Biographical
Introductions]

December 16—One of the reasons I don't like big parties is
that I'm seldom at ease in the presence of strangers. Thrust
abruptly into a position of intimate social contact with a
man or woman who is no more than a vaguely muttered
name to me, I get nervous. I get nervous because I have a
long sordid history of embarrassments growing out of a positive talent for saying the wrong thing. The fault lies, I think,
in the methods by which people are introduced to one
another.

More or less as a joke I have, for some years, flown
violently in the face of convention and insisted that whenever I am invited to a dinner party I am entitled to ask two
questions before accepting. The first: "What you having to
eat?" And the second, much more important: "Who else is
gonna be there?"

It has become almost a vital matter for a guest to know
who else is gonna be there. Yet it is not considered genteel

for a hostess to forewarn and forearm one guest against the presence of another. It is not even polite for the hostess, when she is performing the introductions, to furnish any clues.

Arriving at a party where the company may add up to a dozen or more, the victim is led round the circle. "Mr. Blodgett, meet Mr. Caraway. Howjado. Mrs. Williams, this is Mr. Caraway. Howjado. Mr. Cleewhorts, Mr. Caraway. Happy to meet you." And so on, swiftly and efficiently, to the end of the line. The brain swims, the senses blur, and the confusion is not unlike that which prevailed at the Battle of Hastings.

After that comes clumping. We get off in little clumps and sometimes there are only two persons in a single clump. Mr. Blodgett, perhaps, and Mrs. Williams. "Isn't Dolly a marvelous hostess?" says Mrs. Williams. "Utterly charming," agrees Mr. Blodgett. "Have you," says Mrs. Williams, "ever tasted those wonderful stuffed pork chops she does?" There is a sound of neck-knuckles cracking as Mr. Blodgett's head jerks back and a chill settles over the conversation. How was Mrs. Williams to know that Mr. Blodgett is a vegetarian, that he regards the mere act of stuffing a pork chop to be a barbaric crime against nature?

Full scale wars have been started by lesser incidents.

℃

Years back I attended a Christmas party at which a foreign correspondent, just back from Europe, was holding the center of attention with his analysis of The Situation. Quite frankly I was envious of him; all the women were hanging on this blowhard's every word and nobody was paying a bit of heed to *my* opinions, either foreign or domestic. I found myself standing next to a handsome man who was a complete stranger to me and so, in fairly vigorous tones, I began telling him about the *true* state of affairs in Europe as well as the Far East. He listened intently, nodding and smiling and occasionally saying, "Very interesting," and even, "Quite sound." At length, after I had made a particularly wild observation about the secret schemings of the Cambodians, he murmured: "An extremely provocative thought. Mind if I repeat it to my class tomorrow?"

"Your class?" I said. "You mean you *teach?*"

"Yes," he said. "At Columbia."

I swallowed a couple of times and then, all the authoritative timbre gone from my voice, asked, "What's your subject?"

"Political science," he said. It turned out that he was one of the nation's foremost authorities on international affairs, a man who would soon have an important role in the organization of the United Nations and who later would succeed Eisenhower as president of Columbia. His name was Dr. Grayson Kirk.

Once at a party in Arizona I met another handsome man who expressed some curiosity about my work as a writer, and I told him all about it in large detail, explaining about first drafts and revisions, how to put a publisher in his place, the functions of the semicolon, how to use carbon paper, and so on. *He* turned out to be Erskine Caldwell, one of the most widely read authors of our time.

There have been other moments, equally embarrassing, and they could have been avoided if the hostess in each instance had been just a trifle more specific in her introductions. The blame lies with the etiquette books. Those books ordain that people should never be billboarded, that a hostess who identifies each of her guests is boorish and crude and unmannerly. Emily Post declares firmly that a hostess "who exploits her friends as though she were the barker at a side-show is a bore no less than a pest."

Mrs. Post allows only one type of information to be conveyed in party introductions—that of family relationship. It is perfectly genteel for the hostess to say, "Meet Mr. Blodgett, my second cousin," or "This is Mrs. Whitter, my sister-in-law." I can only assume that this information is a sort of warning to me against making any unseemly cracks about the hostess in the presence of her kinfolks. If that be true, I think it's even more important that I be told where Mr. Blodgett stands on the matter of meat. A vegetarian might be much more sensitive about pork chops than about his second cousin.

In spite of all the talk we hear about conformity, the world is full of people who have stout prejudices and many of these people are willing and even eager to voice those prejudices in public. This produces a powder-keg situation at parties where one guest doesn't know the identity of another guest. If I tell a man at a party that the V. & R. Railroad is a rattletrap collection of mismanaged scrap iron I'm almost certain to find out later that I've been addressing the chairman of the Board of the V. & R. If I cuss out a certain television commerical it's a sure thing that among my listeners is the man who not only wrote that commerical but won a bronze plaque and a trip to Bermuda for doing it. If I denounce a specific community as a quagmire of political corruption, I'm very likely talking to the mayor of that city.

The horror works equally well in reverse. I once fell into conversation with a lady who began asking me a series of enigmatical questions concerning ghosts, reincarnation and ectoplasmic manifestations. I found out later that she was under the impression she was talking to Thorne Smith, the author of *Topper* and *Turnabout*.

☺

Some social arbiters recommend that an efficient dinner hostess should keep a card index on all guests and potential guests, listing their likes and dislikes. Let us assume that Mr. Cleewhorts is about to spend a weekend at the Whitter house. Mrs. Whitter digs out his card. "Troy Cleewhorts. Bachelor. Doesn't like to be called 'Troy' but prefers nickname 'Piggie.' Left-handed. Won't eat kidneys. Favors Old Noggin-Throb bourbon mixed half-and-half with Dr. Pepper, dash of soy sauce. Hates tiny ash-trays. Enjoys a banana with his beer. At best when talking about his immunity from poison ivy. Put tranquillity pills on bed table."

Such a dossier is quite sensible but I would like to recommend that it be expanded with further background material, and that it be put to its maxium effective use. Note should be made of Piggie Cleewhorts' political and religious beliefs, nature of employment, any physical defects, hobbies, state in which he was born (especially if it's Texas) and such other information as might be pertinent.

Then, when the hour for the party arrives, the cards of each guest should be spread on a table in the foyer for all to inspect. "Look, George," says Mrs. Blodgett, "look here what it says about this Mr. Craley. He stands on his head for half an hour every morning before breakfast. And get this! It says he favors shooting the Secretary of State. Now, for heaven's sake don't tell him how the Secretary put you through law school."

There's only one drawback to this plan. The hostess would have trouble getting her guests out of the foyer. I, for one, would want to spend the evening with those intimate little biographies. And if the hostess should announce that dinner was served, I'd ask if I might bring a batch of the cards to the table with me.

Emily Post, I'm sure, would never agree to the card scheme. Yet I think she might unbend a little and permit a hostess to identify her guests graciously and without making the information offensive. Just recently at a small dinner party in my own home I introduced an English lady to Mrs. Don Briggs. Somewhat later I became conscious of the fact that the English lady was giving Mrs. Briggs a lecture on the state of the American theater, telling her which shows were good and which were bad, delving at questionable length into theatrical history and lore, treating of various techniques in dramaturgy. I have never seen a person so deeply embarrassed as that English lady when she found out that Mrs. Don Briggs was Audrey Christie, who has been active in the American theater since she was fifteen years old. And it was all my fault. During the introduction I could easily have said, "Surely you remember Audrey Christie in *The Voice of the Turtle*." And I could have added, just in case the English lady thought *The Voice of the Turtle* was the name of a London pub, "Great li'l ole actress, Audrey!"

The hostess of today is not lacking in professional advice on how to entertain successfully. She's taught to be meticulous in the smallest of details, e.g., the fat end of the toothpick should be uppermost when thrust through a miniature frankfurter. I think she should be permitted to identify her guests, one to another, at least so far as their professions are concerned. If the rules aren't changed, then I've got to find another solution—either that or quit going to parties.

One way out would be to take matters into your own hands. Confront the stranger boldly and give him a fill-in on yourself. Say, "I'm Carl Clinkinfuss. I happen to be a tree surgeon. Of all the trees in the world, I like the sugar maple the best. That's my wife over there by the fireplace. She's a backslid Rosicrucian. You might not notice it but she's got a wooden leg. It's ash." If you could say that much you'd be saying quite a bit and before long your companion would surely tell you a few things about himself as well as about his wife.

Some years ago I read that Clare Boothe Luce has a nice gambit for getting a conversation going at a party. Finding herself seated next to a stranger, she says, "Now, tell me all about that fascinating job of yours!" Through this simple device Mrs. Luce soon learns everything she needs to know about her companion.

I decided that the Luce technique was exactly the thing I was seeking. But, as I've suggested, the breaks seem to go against me. The very next time I found myself involved with a stranger at a party, I switched on my smile of charm and said to him, "Now, tell me all about that fascinating job of yours."

He turned and gave me a long, quizzical look. Then he said, "I'm an undertaker."

<hr>

Maid's Day Off

December 17–Let's come back, just a moment, to the matter of Thursday—traditionally the servants' day off.

There is a well-to-do couple living near us and employing a man and wife as cook and butler. The servants are English, and quite proper, and Mr. and Mrs. K—— never misbehave in front of them. Surely they never quarrel, or even raise their voices in anger. No. They save it all up till Thursday. All the grievances, large and small, are preserved until that day when the servants are off, and then Mr. and Mrs. K—— go at each other like wild dogs. I have been told that Mrs. K—— keeps a list, all week long, of the things that have made her angry, and when Fightin' Day comes, she holds the list in her hand and unleashes her rage item by item.

Another neighbor is a man who considers himself highly cultured; he has no use for television and frequently says so. "Wouldn't allow one of the things in my house," he declares. He, too, has live-in servants and some years ago had to buy *them* a TV set. He complained about it, all over the neighborhood, saying television should be outlawed. Lately, however, he has been showing evidence of having been looking at the screen. He talks about certain television shows and he has even been known to speak favorably of some. Several of us have finally, in the manner of Sherlock Holmes, figured it out. The only TV shows he knows anything about are those scheduled Thursday evenings. He can talk glibly about Thursday night performers, but knows nothing of those who appear the other six nights of the week. It is clear. He still refuses to have a set in his part of the house but on Thursday evenings, when his servants are away, he sneaks into their quarters and just has himself one hell of a time.

> Somebody ought to write a book called "What
> Every OLD Man Should Know."
> *–Sayings of Avery*

The Brain-pickers

[Why Pay for Advice?]

December 21–There were about thirty guests at our own Christmas cocktail party last night, and as the host I was under instructions to circulate, to keep moving from cluster to cluster, to make certain that no one was suffering for want of sustenance. I was performing my assignment to the best of my ability and trying, at the same time, to keep an eye on Dr. Ferdinand Wake. He's one of the best doctors in our area and I wanted to draw him aside and ask him something. Nothing real important. Just that ache in my left shoulder. Normally it didn't bother me except when my arm was elevated at a certain angle. It wasn't really worth *going* to a doctor about. I figured Dr. Wake would be able to tell me in one sentence whether it was neuralgia or bursitis or just a strained muscle. A question that could be answered in one second . . . it would be ridiculous to go all the way down to the village and sit in a doctor's ante-room for thirty minutes just to get that small opinion.

I saw him once standing off in a corner with Mrs.

Clackett and she was bending his ear assiduously while he was staring vacantly into his glass. I noticed that at one point she stepped back and used her index finger to describe a small circle on her own body, just above the hip bone. And at that moment Rube Anders, the lawyer, called out across the room to Dr. Wake and the doctor moved briskly over to the group where Anders was standing.

A few minutes later the doctor came bustling up to me. He glanced at his watch and said he had an important call to make at the hospital and before I could say a word about my shoulder he was gone.

Five minutes later Bob Wingate, the architect, took his departure.

Three minutes after that lawyer Rube Anders left.

I didn't think much about it at the time; there are always people who drop in at cocktail parties for courtesy's sake and then go on to other appointments. The rest of the crowd had settled down to the droning buzz that is characteristic of all such functions and as the clock moved along that buzz grew, by slow degrees, louder and louder. Finally I got a signal from the girl who was working in the kitchen. I had misjudged on gin.

I hurried out and got in the car and drove down to Hobe Renner's tavern in North Patent. The moment I walked through the tavern door I saw them—Dr. Wake, Bob Wingate and Rube Anders, sitting at a table in the back corner of the room. I walked over to them.

"What's the matter?" I asked. "Afraid you'll get poisoned up at my place?"

They were a little sheepish at first and then Bob Wingate spoke up. "I'm sorry," he said, "but I couldn't take it any more. That dame with all the blue lace, the one who lives up the road from you, was trying to drag me away from the party. Wanted me to run over to her house with her and look at her attic—tell her what I thought about partitioning off one end of it for a guest room. And then your wife . . . no, I'd better not say it."

Rube Anders stared at the architect for a moment, then turned to me. "Sit down a minute," he said, and then to Wingate, "Go ahead and tell him—we've got to explain why we ran out on him."

"Your wife," said Wingate, "was trying to pull me away from the attic woman. Your wife wanted me to tell her the correct position for a picture window there in your living room."

Dr. Ferdinand Wake cleared his throat.

"I don't mind telling you," he said, "that I hate cocktail parties. I never stay more than ten or fifteen minutes and even then I always get stuck. That Clackett woman was trying to get a complete diagnosis of a pain that comes and goes in her side. And that writer friend of yours, Mabry, was pestering me about his cousin's sciatica. He stood there with a straight face and told me that his cousin had sciatica so bad that he couldn't sleep nights, and what would I recommend to ease it. Now, tell me the truth. Does Mabry have sciatica?"

"Yes," I said. "I don't understand why he'd tell you it was his cousin."

"It's almost always somebody's cousin," said Rube Anders, "except in the case of your neighbor Forwood. He dragged me clear out to the front stoop to ask me if servants can be used as witnesses to a will. He said he was just curious about it, that his sister-in-law was involved in a will contest in New York."

"That's funny," I said. "I know Forwood pretty well. I never heard that he had a sister-in-law."

"Of course he doesn't have a sister-in-law," said Anders.

Dr. Wake had been sitting quietly, nursing his drink. Now he spoke.

"I've been thinking," he said, "that we professional men ought to have more courage. Like Dr. Crothers. There's a man I admire. For years he's been going to dinner regularly at Sam Miller's house over back of McLain Street. You know Sam Miller—I imagine he's got more money than anybody else around here. He has three grown children living on the place and half a dozen grandchildren. Dr. Crothers goes to dinner there every other Saturday night. And one by one, every member of that family, at some point during the evening, starts talking symptoms and wheedling advice out of Crothers. He got fed up with it. A couple of months ago he arrived as usual at Miller's house but this time he walked in with his bag in his hand. He called the whole family together. 'Now,' he says, 'everybody line up.' Eleven Millers lined up in front of him and he went down the line, saying, 'Now, what's wrong with *you?*' He insisted that they recite all their ailments, and he advised and prescribed, and then when it was over he says, 'Examination's over. Let's not hear any more about aches and pains for the rest of the evening.' It was one of the most sensible things a doctor ever did."

"Do you mean," I put in, "that all three of you are subjected to this sort of thing whenever you go out socially?"

"Always," said Rube Anders.

"And forever," said Wingate.

"I can't go to a party," said Anders, "or even to someone's house for a quiet dinner, without somebody asking me for a legal opinion of one kind or another. Let me tell you a little story."

"Go ahead," I said, pulling out the scratch pad I usually carry in my coat pocket. "I think this whole thing is outrageous. I think I'll try to write something about it—maybe put all these people to shame."

℄

Anders said he was sitting over at the country club one afternoon when Jamie Bascom sat down beside him. Jamie's got one of the big automobile agencies up here. Jamie started telling Rube Anders about a snarl he was in over a lease on the building where he runs his business. He wanted to know, in a casual sort of way, what he ought to do. Rube Anders told him what he thought he ought to do. A few weeks later the two men met on the street.

"Anders," said Jamie Bascom, with more than a touch of asperity, "I just want you to know that I did what you told me to do about that lease, and everything turned out wrong. You couldn't have suggested a worse course."

"Well, Jamie," said Anders, "the advice I gave you was worth exactly what you paid for it."

Both Dr. Wake and Bob Wingate roared with laughter, and I made a note about the Jamie Bascom matter.

"I can beat that one," said Wingate. "There's a Mrs. Coningsby lives on an estate up near Katonah. She's a great bridge player and one day she drew what she considered to be a remarkable bridge hand. She thought she played it perfectly, but she wasn't sure. So she sat down and wrote a letter to Fenwick, the big bridge expert in New York. She described the hand and told how she had played it, and asked him if she had played it correctly—if he could detect any flaw in her strategy. A few days later she got a letter back from him. He said it was truly a remarkable hand and that she had played it exactly right—he couldn't improve on what she had done with it. And he enclosed a bill for a hundred dollars."

"Good for him!" said Dr. Wake.

"Well, sir," Wingate continued, "she was pretty indignant about it. She decided she simply would refuse to pay it. She'd let him sue her before she'd pay it. But she was quite disturbed about it. A week or so later she got on an afternoon train for New York and found herself sitting alongside Ev Greer. You know Ev Greer—big New York lawyer, has a place at Katonah. Well, Mrs. Coningsby knew Ev Greer and they talked a while about the parkway extension and then she told him about that bill she got from Fenwick. She said she thought it was highway robbery—after all, he hadn't given her any advice; he only told her that she had played the hand correctly. She wanted to know what Ev Greer thought of such an outrage. Ev said, 'You knew he was an expert. You knew that he makes his living as a bridge expert. I don't see that you've got an out. I think you'd better pay him.' And the following day she got a bill for a hundred dollars from Ev Greer."

Dr. Wake laughed so hard at this one that I thought he was going to have a stroke. When he finally regained his composure, he addressed himself to me.

"You can't appreciate," he said, "how rough it can really be on doctors. Dentists, too. Did you ever have a dentist at a party at your house? Well, invite one some day. Keep an eye on him. I'll make you a bet that before the party's over someone will get him aside, open his mouth wide, and start pointing to teeth."

"It's brutal," said Rube Anders. "The whole world is populated by brain-pickers."

"And you," said Dr. Wake, leveling a finger at me, "are a professional brain-picker. What are you doing now? You're picking our brains. You go around picking everybody's brains. So don't pretend you're sympathetic."

I hadn't thought of it that way, but it was true. I remembered several occasions when I had asked both Dr. Wake and Rube Anders for technical information on some subject I was writing about. I was thinking about it, a little shamefully, when Dr. Wake stood up and walked from the table to the bar.

"Good Lord," I said, "he's not sore at me, is he?"

"Of course not," said Rube Anders, glancing toward the doctor. "He's just gone over there to talk to Henry Caffey."

"Who's Henry Caffey?"

"Plumber."

"Well," I said, "I've got to get on my way." I went to the bar to ask Hobe Renner if he could let me take two or three bottles of gin. Hobe said he couldn't sell them to me, but he'd make me a present of them if my birthday was anywhere near. He was putting them in a bag when I overheard part of the conversation down the bar. Henry Caffey was talking to Dr. Wake.

"Tell you, Doc," he said, "it's usually the little wire that hooks onto the ball-plunger. That wire gets bent and throws the plunger out of line. Just fool around with that wire—keep bending it till the plunger drops straight. Then you won't have to jiggle 'er any more."

"Fine," said Dr. Wake. "I'll try that. Much obliged to you, Henry."

I took my bag and got in the car and started home, feeling a little better about things in general.

The High Bid of Mrs. L——

December 29—Our neighbor Mrs. L—— goes to auctions. She's really insane about them, and she often buys things for which she has no use. God designed her as a favor to auctioneers. If an auctioneer is at all persuasive, he can sell her anything and at almost any price. Just yesterday she went to a big auction at the Carey estate and she began bidding on a huge desk which the late Mr. Carey had used all his adult life. It was a beautiful and expensive piece of furniture and there was really no place for it in Mrs. L——'s house, but she kept bidding and the price got up to four hundred dollars and then she bid four hundred and fifty. The auctioneer stepped up the tempo of his pitch, and put a throb in his voice, and went into another ecstatic description of the desk. Mrs. L—— was high bidder of the moment and it looked as if she would win out, but the auctioneer made one last try, saying the desk was a criminal steal at four hundred fifty, look at the beauty of that oak, the magnificence of that green leather, and Mrs. L—— was so overcome that she suddenly cried out, "Five hundred!", and the gavel fell. She had even outbid herself.

Stiff Neck

January 3—Jack Wheeler, the veteran newspaper syndicate man, who tried to introduce his tenant farmer to Plato, lives over near the Connecticut border. We were spending New

Year's Eve there last week and Mrs. Wheeler told me how they happened to get married.

"We both lived in Yonkers years ago, and we knew each other but I never dreamed of marrying Jack. He had a job on a newspaper in Manhattan and he drove back and forth in one of the early-model Fords. One winter night he left his office and got in his car and couldn't get it moving. He soon found out that it would operate in reverse gear but it wouldn't go forward. In those days garages were few and far between, so Jack just put that car in reverse and backed *all the way to his house in Yonkers*. At least fifteen miles. It was bitter cold but he drove backwards all the way with his head stuck out so he could look behind him. When he arrived his head was fixed in that position and he couldn't move it. They called a doctor and the doctor took Jack's head in both hands and gave it a hard, grinding twist and got it back where it belonged. I saw him do it. And I said to myself, that's the kind of man I'd like to marry. And I did."

Later I asked Jack if the story were true and he growled: "She always gets things wrong. It wasn't a Ford, it was a Chalmers."

> If you ever hear a man say he doesn't like a
> Cadillac, put him down as a person of violent
> opinions—most of them wrong.
>
> —*Sayings of Avery*

Dermatology

[Baldness Can Be Beautiful]

January 12–Judging from the amount of space devoted to it
in the press, we are being led to believe that photography
has been perfected as an art form. I am here to argue the
contrary. The modern camera, in spite of all the mysterious
"improvements" of the last twenty years, falls down on the
job when it tries to cope with head-hair.

I have been aware of this imperfection in cameras for
several years. Whenever I look at myself in a mirror I can
see plainly enough that my hair is holding its own quite
well, that I really don't have the appearance of a man growing bald. Yet whenever I have my picture taken, the image
turns out to be that of a man whose most distinctive feature
is his fading hairline.

When I first discovered that the cameras, both movie
and still, were not picking up certain hairs that exist on the
forepart of my scalp, I considered the possibility that my
mirror might be lying to me.

I drove over to see my neighbor Avery. I knew a secret

about him. A year or so ago a prominent comic-strip artist in New York, a man grown quite bald, began telling his friends that he had discovered a miraculous method for growing hair on an empty head. He simply washed his scalp every day with yellow laundry soap and he was going about town boasting about it and demanding that people inspect the fuzz that had appeared on his head. The Broadway columnists made mention of his "discovery" and in no time at all there was a boom in yellow laundry soap from coast to coast. Avery was one of those who tried it. The way I knew about it, his cleaning woman told the Pennell's gardener and he told the milkman and the milkman told Charlie Blair and he told me. Avery, I might add, got no fuzz.

We walked into his living room and I asked him to stand in front of the big mirror that hangs over his fireplace.

"Does it look to you," I said, "as if you had a pretty good growth of hair?"

"Certainly," he said. "Are you trying to insinuate that I'm getting bald?"

I'm not one to deliberately wound a man's vanity but, to be truthful, Avery is thinning out.

"Not at all," I said. "I'm just investigating an optical illusion. When I look in a mirror I can see plenty of hair. But when somebody takes my picture, it looks like I'm getting bald."

"I've noticed the same thing," said Avery. "It's the damn cameras they put out nowadays. Give me the old-time box camera, cost a couple of bucks, took an honest picture that showed a man's hair. However, in your case . . ." He looked at my head and hesitated.

"Go ahead," I said.

"In your case," he said, "I think the way your hair looks in a mirror can be explained. It's a matter of angles, and the way your eyes set in your head—makes you look like you've got more hair than you've actually got. That is, it makes it look that way to *you*."

I didn't want to get into a quarrel with him. I simply said, "Avery, I've got more hair growing out of my ears than you've got on your whole head. And I'll tell you why. I wash my ears every day with yellow laundry soap. Good . . . *bye!*"

Considerably upset, I returned home and stood again in front of the mirror, resigned to accept the truth if it were revealed to me. It was. I had hair. Not a great, wild, bushy, Einsteinian sunburst of hair, but a good and sufficient amount. The mirror does not lie. The camera is the villain.

ℂ

This whole experience led me to do some profound thinking on the plight of men who actually *are* growing bald. There is much talk nowadays about the emancipation of the human male from stiff and uncomfortable clothing. Regardless of what the etiquette ladies may think of it, men are now turning up at semi-fashionable parties wearing foam rubber on their feet, pastel slacks, shirts whose patterns might have been copied from a housepainter's dropcloth, and sometimes no neckties.

There are a few Old Guard dissenters but most of us consider this revolution a good thing. It represents a major change in attitude and the social historians of the future will have to deal with it in the event there is a future. Yet this revolution is not complete. It extends only from the soles of the feet to the Adam's apple. It needs to spread upward and take in the scalp. It is my own opinion that the change in clothing styles has been wrought by the men themselves. It is up to the men, then, to alter the world's thinking on the subject of hair. The time has come to recognize the slick fact that baldness can be beautiful.

Understand, now, I'm not arguing this matter from a selfish point of view. I've got hair, plenty of hair, all the hair I need. Naturally I don't have as much as I had ten years ago. Nobody does, including Lassie. A little bit of my frontal thatch may have disappeared, just enough to inspire vulgar remarks from certain of my fair-weather friends.

Just recently I sat in a chair while a television make-up girl worked on my face. She had been hanging around studio wise-guys so long that she fancied herself as a wit. She said, for example, "This wrinkle you got right here, I may have to put some putty in it." And then she giggled. A real kay-rackter!

I put her out of my mind and began concentrating on witticisms I would utter once the program was on the air. Then suddenly I realized that she was doing something to my scalp. I glanced in the mirror and saw that she had a thing like an eyebrow pencil with which she was stroking black lines on the forepart of my skull.

"Hey," I said, "what're you doing?"

She made an effort to be tactful. "I'm just trying to take the shine off," she said. "Your hair is getting *just a trifle* thin here in the front and if I don't put these lines in and smudge it up, it will really look worse than it is."

Around TV studios everybody, but *everybody*, is always making with the yocks.

"Young lady," I said, "you get yourself a rag and erase all those black lines immediately. It happens I have enough hair to suit my own taste and I'm not going on this program with my scalp all phonied up."

She gave me an argument, but my sense of honesty and fidelity prevailed and finally she rubbed out the black lines.

A couple of days later I had a letter from a comical friend in Chicago saying, "Caught you on TV. Boy, you're beginning to look like an overripe casaba." (He's now off my Christmas card list.) The eternal ribbing that bald or balding men have to take is a blot on our national culture. It's as if there were something wrong, even disgraceful, about baldness. Those of us whom Nature has endowed with an amplitude of hair owe it to our fellow men to step in and do something about it. I have become so convinced that a bald head is so much more attractive than a mop of hideous hair that I may, any day now, simply yank out all the hair I have in the middle and then start off on a career as a rake.

I have been trying to find, in history and philosophy, some support for my theory that a bald-headed man is essentially a better man than one with a lot of hair—even one with more hair than I've got. At first the search was discouraging, for I started with a book of universal proverbs. The heathen Chinese have one which goes, "Of ten bald men nine are deceitful and the tenth is stupid." And the Czechs say, "A good man grows gray, but a rascal grows bald." It is astonishing how childlike some foreigners can be.

The Englishman, Thomas Dekker, once exclaimed in print: "How ugly is a bald pate! It looks like a face wanting a nose." This Thomas Dekker's own scalp is said to have had the nubby touch. History tells us he was a man who didn't pay his debts.

There was a strong prejudice against baldness in ancient Rome. Bald Romans wore wigs on the theory that they matched up nicely with those ridiculous togas, and the reason Julius Caesar wore that laurel wreath on his head was to conceal his baldness. Yet here in antiquity we find a glimmer of encouragement. It is recorded that the Emperor Caligula once ordered that the bald-headed men be separated from the hair-headed men among the hundreds of political prisoners and criminals in the dungeons. Then he had the bald-headed men thrown into the arena, and eaten up by wild beasts (of which he was one). Some historians say that this was just an idle whim on the part of the Emperor. Others say that Caligula operated on the theory that bald-headed men were easier to eat. I dispute both of these arguments. I say he was scared. He realized that bald-headed men are much more intelligent than hairy men and that the bald prisoners might outwit their jailers and get loose and throw him in the Tiber with a chunk of Carrara marble tied to his neck.

The theory that bald men are smarter than others is supported by science. In 1948 a brilliant man, Dr. R. E. G. Armattoe of Londonderry, wrote a report to the American Association of Physical Anthropologists. Dr. Armattoe described himself as a student of hair. He had conducted an extensive survey which proved that most intellectual men are apt to be bald. For quite a while he went around examining the scalps of eggheads. He attended a meeting of the British Association for the Advancement of Science and, hanging from the rafters, counted bald heads. He found that fifty-five per cent of the delegates showed "central baldness" and twenty-two per cent showed "frontal baldness." On another occasion he examined the scalps of all the Swedish intellectuals he could locate and found that seventy per cent of them were bald. I say the time draws near when we will bow down before bald-headed men, and respect and venerate them as superior creatures.

☺

There remains an aspect of this question that, quite frankly, has me disturbed. Throughout history men have been prone to cover up their baldness with wigs. In the Roman Empire they even had hair *painted* on their scalps. The good philosopher Martial protested against this silliness, saying, "There is nothing more contemptible than a bald man who pretends to have hair."

In our own time the use of the wig or "hairpiece" is growing at an alarming rate. For a long while the public has known that stage and motion picture actors, who are bald or growing bald, have affected hairpieces. We cannot quarrel with them. They are *playing a part*. They are undertaking the roles of younger men and it is altogether ethical for them to have a "rug" or "divot" glued to their scalps.

In television, however, the practice is becoming offensive. More and more announcers and commentators are putting on hairpieces. I am acquainted with a man who appears frequently on the TV screen as an announcer. He hasn't much hair left in front, yet he has always looked quite handsome and dashing to me. He went along for a few years with his head *au naturel* and then just recently, some hairy-headed producer talked him into wearing a scalp-doily. I saw him the first night he appeared with it. He looked as if he had just engaged in a butting contest with a grizzly bear. To my esthetic eye, all his masculine beauty disappeared. He had been, before, an attractive man in a slick, glistening sort of way. I simply don't understand why he changed. We work our fingers to the bone waxing floors and furniture and automobiles to give them the deep luster and sheen that makes for beauty; but let a man's scalp glow and glisten and people apparently think there is something degrading about it.

We hear now and again of complaints about men who appear on public beaches with their chests exposed. These protests, usually from women, are directed against those men who have thick jungle growths of rich black hair on their bodies. It is revolting, say the complainants; it is disgraceful, and even sickening. Yet it is only hair, and if it were transferred to the bald pate of another man, the same women would delight in running their fingers through it. Hair's hair.

So I repeat—it is time we men who have an abundance of hair do something on behalf of those whose hair has disappeared. It has been demonstrated that they've got superior brains and that they are intrinsically handsomer than the rest of us.

There has been only one incident in all of universal history in which a bald head has brought tragedy to its owner. Aeschylus, the father of Greek tragic drama, was sitting one day in the Athenian sun. An eagle with a tortoise in his claws came circling overhead. His eye caught the glint of the philosopher's head, he maneuvered into position and dropped the tortoise. The blow shattered both the shell of the tortoise and the skull of Aeschylus. The ironical part of this tragic drama was that the eagle had no knowledge of what he had done. He flew down and scooped up his tortoise meat and as he soared skyward again he remarked to himself, "Nice rocks around here."

❦

Cure for Hiccups

January 25—It was some years ago that I decided to take up gardening on a small scale and bought several books of instruction, resolving that I would never deviate from advice of the experts. One of the first things I read was a bit of instruction

on how to sow seed. The book said it was not a simple operation—that you only learned it through practice. "Before you
venture into the garden," it said, "spread a newspaper on the
floor, then get a handful of sand, and practice sowing it in
orderly rows on the newspaper." I got a newspaper and spread
it on the floor and was about to start outdoors to get some
sand when a thought entered my mind. Suppose someone,
maybe Mr. Buttolph, walked in while I was down on all fours
sowing sand on a newspaper. I'm self-conscious about such
things, and embarrass easily. And I remembered that day
during the first spring when I was sitting in the living room
reading *The Old Farmer's Almanac*. I came to an item about
hiccups. It said that a sure cure for the hiccups involved putting the thumbs on either side of the nose, blocking the air
passage tightly, and at the same time placing the little fingers
over the ear passage. Then swallow three times.

I didn't have the hiccups at that moment, but I put my
thumbs against my nose, and stretched my little fingers until
I got the ear passage closed, and I was swallowing quite
elaborately when a voice sounded dimly in the room:

"Mr. Smith! What's happened!"

A high school girl, friend of my daughter's, had walked
into the room, taken one look at me, and decided I was either
committing suicide or dying a natural death acrobatically. I
tried to laugh it off and said I had just been reading about this
crazy hiccup cure. But I feel certain that little jerk-ess blabbed
it all over town and probably even went through the performance she had caught me in.

So I didn't sow any sand on a newspaper.

A fellow who's inclined to spit a lot shouldn't keep a dog.

–Sayings of Avery

Christmas Camera

[Education of a Movie Producer]

February 2–At Christmastide members of my family, full of admiration and love for me, pooled their resources and gave me a nice camera for taking color movies and a projector for showing them on a screen. I was genuinely touched, for several reasons. I had never in all the previous years of my life ever gone in for photography of any sort, and had no ambition to do so, hence the gift was a thoughtful one. Secondly, the resources which had been pooled were just sufficient to pay for a screen, so they charged the camera and projector to my account. And thirdly, as it turned out, I am the only member of the family able to operate the camera with any degree of efficiency, so practically all the pictures are of *them* and there are precious few of me for posterity to look at.

Nonetheless I appreciated the spirit and generosity with which the gift was tendered and I went to work shooting movies. At the very beginning I spoke a thunderous resolution. From bitter experience I know that the greatest bore of the twentieth century is the man who hauls out his projector and begins showing home movies to people who have never done a mean thing to him in their lives. I resolved, out loud, that I would never show my films to anyone. That is, unless the demand were both insistant and sincere. People would have to plead with me, and plead convincingly, before I'd ever set up that projector. I must confess that in weak moments I have violated my rule several times, but only in special cases where the guests involved were acquainted with me personally.

One week-end during the early part of last month, two young men named John and Dan came out from the city for a visit. I had known them since they were children and now they were grown to manhood and worked together in the offices of a big corporation in New York City.

At the time of their visit I had finished shooting six rolls of film and had put these all together on one big reel. I was fairly itching to show John and Dan the results of my first efforts. I felt that there were certain *very* interesting aspects to my camera work. But I clamped my jaws and held to my resolution. Then one of the boys, Dan, I think, came upon the projector which I had hidden away by placing it in the center of the dining room table.

"Somebody take home movies around here?" he asked casually.

"Yes!" I cried. "I do! Want to look at them?" I didn't wait for his answer but dashed in and started setting up the equipment. I don't even recall that he uttered an answer, yet I had the distinct feeling that inside of him he was simply dying to look at my pictures. While I was threading the film into the projector John came in and, though he didn't say a word, he cast a significant glance at Dan and wiggled his eyebrows Grouchomarxwise, indicating quite clearly that he, too, was eager to inspect my first reel of film. The two of them began talking about their own cameras; I hadn't known it before, but they were amateur photographers, although they were old-fashioned and took nothing but still pictures. Corny.

So I showed them Reel One. It included the following scenes:

1. Wife hanging out wash on a winter day.
2. Dog chasing a red ball.
3. Daughter staring across the hedge, bemused.
4. Wife throwing a snowball, dog chasing it.
5. Buttolphs getting out of their car in driveway.
6. Dog chasing a green ball.
7. Wife shoveling snow.
8. Grown son watching his mother shovel snow.
9. Neighbor kid throwing green ball, dog chasing it.
10. Wife holding grandson with finger in his mouth (grandson's finger).
11. Daughter holding grandson with finger in his mouth.
12. Dog chasing George Shupert.
13. Peters looking wistfully at fir tree.
14. Matson kids drinking cokes in living room.
15. Wife making snowman in yard.
16. Dog chasing Mr. Greer.
17. Estelle Winwood sitting on stone wall.
18. Estelle Winwood throwing ball, dog chasing it.
19. Poinsettia in bloom, wife looking at.
20. Dog chasing Stanley Halle.

Thus it ended, my first full reel of film. I chose to speak quickly, before the boys had a chance to say anything.

"Did you boys, uh, that is, did you notice any technical flaws?"

"You wouldn't mind a little criticism?" spoke up John.

"Oh, not at all! Lord no! I'm just a beginner. Don't know a blessed thing about it. Fire away!" Privately I felt like telling him to get his hat and get off my property. I'd have done it, too, but I was afraid the rat would pull a switchblade knife on me.

"Too much people," he said.

"That's what I thought," put in Dan. "Too much people, and too much dog."

"All you got there," said John, "is just a lot of people."

"Well," I said, concealing my rage, "that's what a movie camera's for, isn't it—taking pictures of people?"

"Look," said Dan patronizingly, "you want to be a good photographer, don't you? You want to take good pictures, don't you?"

"Certainly."

☾

So now they explained all about good photography. They had started out with the same misconceptions, the same false values, that characterized my own beginning. They took pictures of people, and even of an occasional dog. Then the company where they worked announced a prize competition for all the amateur photographers among its employees. First prize was a five hundred dollar government bond. John and Dan entered the contest as a team and after considering many subjects, including people, decided on a photograph of the Manhattan skyscraper where the company had its offices. They experimented quite a bit and finally hit on the idea of standing on the sidewalk and shooting almost straight up to get a real artistic view

[243]

of the building. This was the picture they entered in the competition.

"It was a beaut," said Dan, "but do you know what won?"

"No, what?" I said.

"A picture of a bent nail," said John.

"It was rusty," added Dan. "Just an old bent, rusty nail."

They said that at first they were pretty disgusted about it. They even talked about abandoning the company and looking for jobs in a more intelligent firm. Then an enlargement of the prize-winning picture was put on display in the office, and they studied it at some length.

"We began to see the clean beauty of it," said John.

"It changed our whole approach to photography," said Dan.

"It woke us up," said John.

"Well," I put in, "I'd like to remind you that you're dealing with still photography. *These* happen to be motion pictures."

"Makes no difference at all," said Dan. "Technique's the same. What you've got here is people, people, people."

"And dog, dog, dog," added John.

"But," I protested, "I'm *after* action and movement."

"No," said John. "You just think that's what you're after. You're really after beauty. Now, I think it would be all right for you to do something like, say, a grasshopper. I bet you've got lots of grasshoppers around here in the spring. Get up real close to one. Keep in mind, you don't want him jumping. You want a close-up, a study. Photograph him just standing there. Then you've got something. Not people. Not dogs. Something with *meaning*."

And so I saw the light (diaphragm set at 2.8).

[244]

I began to think in terms of the prize-winning bent nail, and I started looking around for rusty stuff. I bent some nails and watered them and let them lay out for a couple of days. They acquired a fine look of corrosion and I devoted twelve feet of film to their clean beauty. And from this small experiment I went on to further artistic adventures with my camera.

Decadence and disintegration became my theme. I went on the prowl for no-good, worn-out things. If a bent and rusty nail could win a five hundred dollar bond, then I figured there must be merit in uselessness and obsolescence and deterioration. In the attic I found a mildewed first baseman's mitt and I filmed a remarkable study of it, lying on the carpet, mouldering.

I devoted eighteen feet of film to a shrunken potato perched on a brickbat. While I was lining up the atrophied potato, my wife interrupted with a request that I take a shot of a young woman who had just arrived with her new baby. I ridiculed the suggestion. "That's corn," I said. "That's for squares."

She was pretty sore about it. "Well," she said, "if you *must* take pictures of that old potato, I think you ought to have my hand come into the picture, and pick it up, and then throw it, and let the dog chase it."

"Please!" I exclaimed. "You are watching a *long-hair* photographer!"

I ruined a lot of film in my close-up work, but by now I have finished my first full reel of pictures taken in what I call the Bent Nail Motif. The withered potato is included, and the mildewed mitt. I have a sharp study of one half of a pair of scissors, adequately rusted; a mortified fence post, almost consumed by carpenter ants; two burnt matches, lying face to face; a saucer of sludge.

All of this and more is on Reel Two. Every now and then I get it out and run it, and I must confess that it does something to me. And I want everyone to understand that all these shots were taken solely for my own personal satisfaction and enjoyment. I have resolved anew that I will never show them to guests in my house, no matter how much they plead. This time I mean it. I won't even show them to John and Dan. And if you want the unsullied truth, I've resumed taking icky movies of people, people, people. And dog, dog, dog.

———◆———

Dibbles

February 7—I have several books on the fundamentals of carpentry, and a shed full of tools, but I have never undertaken anything in the way of a major construction job. The biggest thing I have built to date is a non-usable sawbuck. In order to build a proper sawbuck it is necessary to mortise two of the crosspieces, else the structure will collapse under a heavy burden. I got out one of the carpentry books and gave myself a lengthy briefing and then went to work. It took me two days to build the sawbuck, most of the time being spent on the mortises. They turned out satisfactorily but the sawbuck didn't. I concentrated so hard on getting those mortises correct that I fumbled the over-all dimensions of the thing. I built it much too low, so that a person trying to saw a log on it would have to bend far over and, after ten minutes of sawing, would need a mortise in his sacroiliac. I still keep that sawbuck around, however, because if it gave me nothing else, it contributed a literary trifle. After I had driven the last nail into it, I stood up and sighed, and then spoke of "the rigors of mortising."

The only other work in creative carpentry that I have attempted was the making of a dibble. A dibble is a gardening instrument used for poking a hole in the ground. I fashioned my dibble from an old broomstick, simply whittling a point on it. It has no metal tip, like dibbles you get in a store. I could have put such a tip on it, but my religion forbids the use of metal tips on dibbles.

---◆◆---

Grommets on a Tarp

February 21—My neighbor Avery is fascinated by technical language, and the other day his eye fell on an advertisement for tarpaulins. The tarps described in the ad were equipped with grommets. The word stuck in Avery's mind and a day or so later, passing the hardware store, he remembered it. He had no need for a tarpaulin but he walked in and said he wanted to buy one. A small one, about eight by twelve. Yes, they had it.

"Has it got grommets on it?" asked Avery.

They assured him that it had grommets on it. They brought it out, packed in a burlap casing. Avery insisted on it being opened. They spread it out on the floor and he stood and looked at it. Then he lifted one corner and peered under it.

"Where's the grommets?" he demanded. "I don't see the grommets."

They showed him—the metal eyelets at each corner.

"Oh," he said. "I didn't notice them before. Light's bad in here."

And he took the tarpaulin, grommets and all, home with him. Now he's looking for something that needs to be covered with a tarpaulin. He'll find something . . . but it won't fit.

Avery's Rule of Three

February 22—Avery is a firm believer in the notion that trouble strikes in series of threes. Yesterday he bought a new shoe-rack which had to be fastened to the inside of a closet door. The closet was in a small hallway immediately outside his bedroom door. He worked and sweated and cussed for two hours and finally got the woodscrews into the ironlike oak of the door, and the shoe-rack was in place. He pushed the door out of the way and gathered up his tools and took them to the basement. Then he went to treat and bandage the two gashes inflicted on his fingers by the demoniacal screwdriver. Now he was ready to survey his handiwork—a job, at last, that had come off pretty well. He walked into the little hallway and swung the closet door open. He stood and stared, his eyes goggling, his mouth agape. *There was no shoe-rack on the door.* It took him a full minute to get himself oriented and to discover that he had fastened the rack to the door of his bedroom.

When he told me about it he tried to laugh it off, but I could tell that he was troubled.

"Boneheads like that," he said, "come in threes. Now I know that the next two handyman jobs I try will go wrong. It always works out that way."

"Well," I said, trying to be comforting, "at least you can look forward to the fourth job—the series of three will be over and the fourth job will turn out all right."

"Not with me it won't," he said. "I finish out a series of three and the next job after that is not the fourth job—it's the start of a brand new series of three."

We were sitting at the time in my toolshed and I found myself feeling just a little sorry for him. It seemed a shame that he should be condemned to one series of three flops right after another series of three failures.

Sitting there thinking about it, I suddenly realized that, no matter what happened with his bedroom shoe-racks and his grommets, I should never feel sorry for him. Avery is, in truth, an admirable man and a man to be envied, for he leads a more exciting and adventuresome life than all of his handy neighbors combined.

A true countryman takes out his pocketknife
to scrape bird dirt off the summer furniture,
then uses the same blade to peel an apple for
himself.

—Sayings of Avery

Neighborly Relations

[Life on the Westchester Frontier]

Feb. 28—I am a citizen of the untamed wilderness, a horny-
handed pioneer living next door to Nature in a harsh land
that has come to be known as Exurbia.

Out here the law of tooth and claw still prevails. We
have not grown soft and flabby, in the manner of city folk.
It is required of us, here on the rough frontier, that we live
by our wits, morning, noon and night.

Just today I was down in the settlement and I observed
the arrival of Mrs. George Skoob, a true pioneer woman. I
noted that she circled the plaza slowly, going around several
times, and then she pulled in and stopped and I went over
and asked if she were in any trouble.

"Nope," she said in her usual forthright manner. "I was
just looking for the meter with the most on it." She had
found one with twenty-two minutes still on it. She always
shops around that way, trying to get the best bargain for
her money. Or, rather, for someone else's money. She ges-

tured toward the meter with its black needle up near the middle point and said grimly, "Dog eat dog."

Out in this semi-civilized land, a good forty miles from New York City, we hold to the survival of the smartest. One of our ladies is called by the name of "bachelor-girl," meaning that she lives alone. It is her belief that she is getting too round and so she has taken to eating a substance called yogurt, thought by the aborigines to evaporate flesh. Whenever one of her friends calls her for a chat on the telephone and asks what she has been doing, she usually replies in disconsolate tones, "Oh, I just sit around here eating my yogurt." Almost always this arouses a flash-flood of sympathy in the heart of the caller, who will say, "Marie, I just can't bear the thought of it—all alone up there with that yogurt. You just forget your darned figure for one evening and get right over here and have dinner with us."

Marie manages to eat heartily two or three times a week by using the yogurt-plus-loneliness ploy. I am happy to say that she learned the trick from me. My wife occasionally goes away to visit relatives for a couple of weeks, leaving me at home alone. Sometimes, as the afternoon wears on and I find myself growing hungry I'll telephone one of the neighbor ladies and say, "Listen, Evelyn, tell me something. When you cook a head of cabbage do you have the water boiling first and then drop it in, or the other way round?" Evelyn, who already knows that I am a temporary bachelor, will respond, "Oh, it really doesn't make much difference about the . . . say, just a minute! What are you doing boiling a whole head of cabbage?" I reply that I am getting ready to cook my dinner. And she almost always says, "Good Lord, you turn that stove off and get in your car and come over here and have dinner with us. We're having fried chicken and there's plenty."

The next night I may work it with another friend, calling up and asking what kind of cheese to cook with macaroni, or what is a medium oven, or how much flour to put in gravy, and so I get invited over to eat steak.

℃

Yes, we have had to learn to use our mother wit here in the wilderness. Conditions are rugged and many of us find it hard to survive on what we are able to scrape from the earth. Take the boys down at the garage. One day it occurred to me that I am forever spilling money out of my pants pocket into the front seat of my car, and some of that money drops down into the crevices. I thought that if I were employed at a garage where people bring their cars in for servicing, the moment the owners departed I would yank out the car seats and look for money. And so I made some inquiries and finally found a mechanic who knew I was not the district attorney. "Oh, sure," he said. "Seat money. That's what we call it—seat money. We got a system of rotating, so each guy gets a car in turn. It becomes a sorta game. My car comes in and I jerk out the seats and find maybe six cents or maybe nothing. So the next car is Charlie's and *he* finds three quarters and two dimes. I keep my wife and me in cigarettes with seat money."

You see? In almost every direction you will encounter people here on the frontier who eke out their miserable existence by toil, stratagem, hook, crook, or little white lie. I have a neighbor whose business is such that people often telephone him at his home in the evenings. He is a shrewd frontiersman and he has worked out a technique for getting rid of these callers. He keeps a bowl of oyster crackers beside his telephone and before picking up the instrument he pops a few crackers into his mouth. If the caller is an unwelcome one, he begins chewing vigorously and noisily, and speaking indistinctly, spitting cracker crumbs, and usually the caller will say, "Oh, you must be having your dinner. I won't bother you now—this thing can wait till tomorrow." And so my neighbor abates a nuisance at the cost of a few oyster crackers. We may be rubes, but we know a trick or two.

I have another neighbor named Bennett who is a lawyer. He has a peculiar hobby—plumbing. Whereas many men are intimidated by U-Bend traps and Fuller-type faucets and compression cock washers, Bennett loves nothing more than to tinker with such things, and usually he knows what he's doing. After I found out about his hobby I worked up a little game. Oh, all right—a little *racket*. Suppose the kitchen sink at my house gets clogged up or springs a leak. I phone Bennett and ask him if he'd like to come by for a drink. Just before he is due at my house, I get out an old rusty wrench I found one day on the road—an enormous wrench that could only be used by sewer builders or oil drillers. I get some black grease and make a few smears on my face and hands, and then muss up my hair, and spread some additional tools and dirty rags around on the floor. Finally, when I hear his car, I put a look on my face as if I were about to bust out crying. In comes Bennett, friendly and vigorous. "What ya doin' there, pal?" he cries out. Then he looks closer and sees that I am trying to cope with a trap beneath the sink. Off comes his coat and he cries, "Put that wrench down! Give me that thing! Stand aside, boy, and leave a *man* go to work!" And in no time at all he has the sink fixed.

Bennett really enjoys those plumbing repairs. The same way that Charlie B. enjoys working with his tube-tester. Several years ago Charlie bought this nice tube-tester for seventy-nine dollars. It is all loaded with dials and leaping needles and outlets and inlets and uplets. Charlie's trouble seems to be that he doesn't have enough tubes to test. On the other hand I have more tubes around my premises than ought to be allowed to one man. I have an electric organ and two TV sets and a hi-fi and various other contrivances which make my house go woof and tweet. Naturally the tubes are always getting out of whack and if I resorted to a professional serviceman each time I have trouble I'd soon be broke. All I have to do is phone Charlie. He comes racing over with his tube-tester and while he's at it, he tests every tube in the house and I have to restrain him from testing the broom. The trick of keeping him happy and contented while he does this job is to follow him around and point at the dials and needles and say, "What's that?" He loves to explain these things, using highly technical terms, and that is part of the fun he gets out of his tube-tester, being able to talk about oscillations and ohms and Slo-Blo fuses and one-quarter ampere pigtail units.

☺

Sometimes, here on the frontier, we discover new procedures (rackets) by accident. You want to hear about my trip to Mexico? You don't? Okay, I'll tell you about it.

One casual telephone call changed my whole life, and for the better. My wife and I had decided we wanted to go on a nice vacation, in some foreign clime, and we had discussed a dozen different possibilities. Then one evening I was reading the local weekly newspaper and saw a three-line item which said, "Mr. and Mrs. C—— M—— of Millwood Road have just returned from a ten thousand mile auto trip through Mexico." That was all. I sat and looked at that item and read it over a few times. It occurred to me that people who have been on a long trip love to talk about it to other people. But an unwritten law has come into being, saying that to talk in detail about your trip is to become a crashing bore. You must never babble about your travels unless people ask you to do it.

Millwood Road is near us and impulsively I got up and looked in the phone book and found their number and called it. I identified myself to Mrs. M—— and apologized for disturbing her, but I said we had been thinking about a trip to Mexico and would they like to come by for cider and tell us something of their experience? Mrs. M—— said better yet, we should come to *their* house for dinner two nights later, and they'd introduce us to some other people who had been to Mexico and loved it and would enjoy talking about it.

And so we went to dinner and there were about twenty people, all Mexico buffs, some with books to lend us, some with pictures they had taken, all with anecdotes and advice.

We traveled to Mexico, and then went back a second time, and even a third, and learned to speak some Spanish and doubled the number of our friends and I wrote a book about our adventures and a story for motion pictures, and learned to play Mexican music on the organ and to cook Mexican food and people began classifying me as an authority on Mexico and sending me books to review and so on and on—all from one impulsive phone call to some people on Millwood Road. If you want to widen your circle, just call up somebody who's been abroad and tell them you'd enjoy hearing all about it.

We on the frontier are rugged individualists, sharper than most people, quick to recognize the main chance.

Know why I was standing down in the settlement today when Mrs. George Skoob came through the plaza shopping for a meter with the most on it? Well, I had gone down to cash a check at the bank, and I had put a penny in the meter for twelve minutes of parking. I twisted the knob and the arrow swung clear over—it must have been a thin penny because I got a dime's worth of time—two hours. It took me but a few minutes to go into the bank and cash my check. When I came out I looked at all the beautiful time on the meter and decided I would loaf around town for a while. I had important work waiting for me at home, but I'm no fool. You think I'd drive away from a meter where I was getting two hours for a penny? Not me! Not anybody else in this community! We have to be just a shade shrewder than the rest of you, and so I stayed downtown the full two hours.

The End